good fish

BECKY SELENGUT

good fish

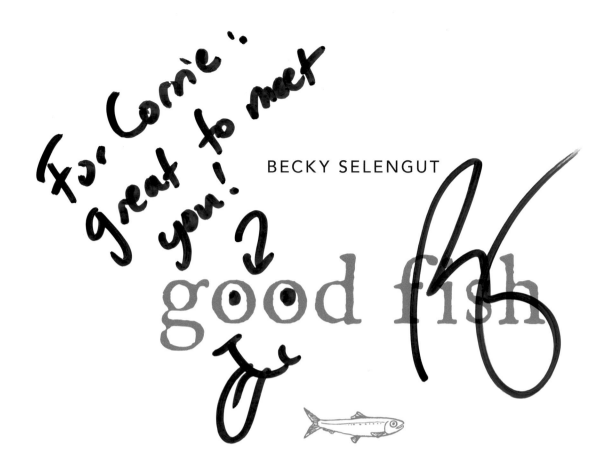

Sustainable Seafood Recipes
from the Pacific Coast

Foreword by Brad Matsen
Wine pairings by April Pogue
Photography by Clare Barboza

SASQUATCH BOOKS
SEATTLE

to dad

Printed in China
Published by Sasquatch Books
17 16 15   9 8 7 6 5 4

Cover photograph: Clare Barboza
Cover design: Anna Goldstein
Interior photographs: Clare Barboza
Interior illustrations: Anna Goldstein
Interior design and composition: Anna Goldstein
Copy editor: Diane Sepanski
Proofreader: Lisa Gordanier

Library of Congress Cataloging-in-Publication Data is available.

ISBN-13: 978-1-57061-662-4
ISBN-10: 1-57061-662-0

Sasquatch Books
1904 Third Avenue, Suite 710
Seattle, WA 98101
(206) 467-4300
www.sasquatchbooks.com
custserv@sasquatchbooks.com

contents

recipe list

LITTLEFISH & EGGS

acknowledgments

To my army of recipe testers, tasters, advisors, and friends, I bow deeply upon one knee: Carrie Kincaid, Heather Diller, Heather Weiner, Becky Ginn, Kim Allen, Maxine Williams, Elaine Hackett, Marc Schermerhorn, David Wiley, Lorna Yee, Henry Lo, Derek Slager, Chris Nishiwaki, Larry Liang, Kristen Ramer Liang, Hans Giner, Catherine Moon Giner, Elaine Mowery, Gordon King, Anna Berman, Shannon and Jason Mullett-Bowlsby, Michael Anderson, Shirley Abreu, Jenise Silva, Matthew Amster-Burton, John Tippett, Allison Day, Gregory Heller, Erika Garcia, Judy Niver, "Oyster Bill" Whitbeck, everyone at Mutual Fish, Nancy Harvey, Shauna James Ahern, Dan Ahern, Amy Duchene, Sue Skillman, Ryan Breske, Hsiao-Ching Chou, Rebekah Denn, Nancy Leson, Janis Martin, Emily Wines, Jake Kosseff, Doug Derham, Miki Tamura, Mona Memmer, Janis Fulton, Therese Ogle, Mimi Southwood, Ba Culbert and the staff at Tilikum Place Café, Susan Actor, Lisa Fisher, Caro Horsfall, Lara Muffley, Melissa Poe, J. Christian Andrilla, Langdon Cook, Rocky Yeh, and the "Food Whores." A big sloppy kiss to Denise Anderson, the queen of recipe testers.

Elizabeth Wales—thank you for sharing your expertise with me, above and beyond that of a good neighbor.

Jill Lightner of *Edible Seattle*, Jackie DeCicco of PCC Cooks, and Giselle Smith of *Seattle Homes and Lifestyles*—each of you makes me a better writer every time I work with you, and I greatly appreciate how supportive you are of my passion for all things seafood (and an occasional missed deadline or five).

They may not be aware of their membership, but the following people are all on my Seafood Advisory Committee; they are fishermen and renowned experts in their fields who have graciously donated their time to advise me on issues of seafood sustainability. Thank you to Jeremy Brown and Rich Childers for your expert review, and to Nick Furman of the Oregon Dungeness Crab Commission. My eternal appreciation to Casson Trenor for your knowledge, passion, love of sushi, and quick pickup on the phone whenever I needed you; Jon Rowley, for inspiring me with all your love and appreciation for the inherent deliciousness of life; Rick Moonen, for being one of the most colorful advocates for the oceans I've ever had the pleasure of meeting—and an incredible chef, to boot; Hajime Sato, for following your heart and taking the huge risk of changing your business in favor of sustainable sushi; Jacqueline Church, for your support and long-standing commitment to sustainable seafood; and Marco Pinchot, for giving so freely of your time and knowledge in guiding our little rat pack on your shellfish-farming tours. Amy Grondin, many thanks for being my go-to fish expert and sustainable seafood compadre for the last four years: you are a generous, knowledge-seeking, fish-lovin' woman; you are the salt of the ocean and have been hugely helpful in getting my facts right for this book.

Amy Pennington, thank you for introducing me to Susan Roxborough, my editor extraordinaire at Sasquatch Books, who brought this idea to my door, appreciated my voice in all its snark (well, maybe not all), and took a chance on giving me so many pages. Thanks to all the folks at Sasquatch, specifically publisher Gary Luke, Rachelle Longé (production editor goddess!), Diane Sepanski (copy editor goddess!), Anna Goldstein (designer goddess!), and Lisa Gordanier (proofreader goddess!).

Clare Barboza, working with you has been like finding a missing limb that looks remarkably like a camera that takes both the shots I imagine in my head but can't produce, and the shots I never had the vision to see in the first place.

Jerry Traunfeld, I consider you my mentor, and it seems fitting that most of this book was written at your restaurant, Poppy, while sitting at the bar drinking a Papi Delicious, tapping away at my computer, and eating some of the most extraordinarily prepared seafood dishes on the Pacific Coast. Thanks to all your staff at Poppy for taking such great care of me and April.

Jeanette Smith and Ashlyn Forshner, my wing(wo)men, you two deserve a week's stay in a spa (yes, I'll rub your feet) for all the help and heart you contributed to this book—it wouldn't be half of what it is without your creativity, humor, and gentle guidance. Food adventures would not be the same without you both.

Mark Malamud, Susan Hautala, and Jasper Malamud, you are my patrons, friends, family, clients, and guinea pigs—your kitchen has been my test kitchen for ten years and counting. This book is as much yours as it is mine.

Some food-and-wine pairings are so sublime that the food makes an already good wine sing, and the wine makes an enjoyable dish unforgettable—and that is precisely how I think of my partnership with April Pogue. Sharing a life of food and wine with April makes everything better.

"We can eat in ways that are good for us AND good for the planet. Instead of feeding our desire for tomatoes 365 days per year, we've rediscovered the joy of summer heirlooms. We're reminded again and again that forcing natural processes into unnatural production has consequences beyond dulling our senses to seasonality. These lessons apply as much to fishing as they do farming. Fish are seasonal, and increasingly, farmed. We can and should enjoy them, in season, responsibly raised or sustainably caught."

—*Jacqueline Church, food writer and sustainable food advocate*

foreword

"One of the great dreams of man must be to find some place between the extremes of nature and civilization where it is possible to live without regret."

—*Barry Lopez*

Twenty-five years ago, a heartbeat in human evolution, we figured out that the sea is not an inexhaustible source of food. Until then, the notion of infinite fish, clams, scallops, oysters, krill, shrimp, and the rest of the ocean banquet was a serviceable fiction that contained a lot of comfort. When I was a kid in the 1950s, the *Weekly Reader* I got in school told me that scientists had determined we could take a billion tons of seafood a year. Mercifully, Thomas Robert Malthus's dreadful calculations that the human population would soon outrun the food supply were wrong. The sea would save us. Whew. By the mid-1970s, slightly better science revised that estimate to about five hundred million tons. Still, no problem at dinnertime. Since most people are no more able to live comfortably with the certain specter of global famine than they are with a firm date for a killer asteroid, those predictions gave us welcome relief. We continued to develop our wide-open fisheries at a breakneck pace. In 1989, though, a couple of decades of careful record-keeping revealed that no matter how many fishermen or how much horsepower we sent to sea, the sustainable yield of food would not be more than a hundred million tons. To that point, fishing and all our interactions with seafood were founded upon the assumption of endless supply, a paradigm that created an economic system dependent on constant development. For a few years after the facts banished the fiction of infinite seafood, we simply blamed the fishermen. Overfishing surely diminished the productive power of the sea and its creatures, but heaping the burden of responsibility on them did not fundamentally alter the calculus of finite seafood and human survival. Finally, we got it.

Becky Selengut's wonderful compendium of sustainable seafood recipes, *Good Fish*, is informed by an indelible truth: we are personally accountable for what we eat. She has taken her inspiration from the acceptance of individual responsibility that finally occurred to us in the early 1990s and continues to build twenty years later. Every one of us should strive to know the home address of the seafood we eat. We should know whether its living relatives are in danger of vanishing forever. We should explore the complexities of eating wild or farmed seafood. Becky has blended the urgency of those demands with exquisite recipes that resonate with her own willingness to embrace the realities of our dependence on the ocean for survival. Last night, when I took my first bite of her seared albacore with ratatouille and caramelized figs, I knew that the fish was line-caught in the Pacific, where albacore are not depleted as they are in the Atlantic. I knew that it was a "Best Choice" on the seafood watch lists of the Monterey Bay Aquarium and the Marine Stewardship Council. I knew it was delicious.

—*Brad Matsen*
Port Townsend, Washington

introduction

I might as well have grown up with pickled herring in my baby bottle. I was weaned just as soon as I could drop my dime-store fishing pole in the big lake that was our backyard. My first real job was down the street at a seafood market in northwest New Jersey, on the shores of Lake Hopatcong. On weekends you'd find me selling crab-stuffed flounder rolls to bridge-and-tunnel businessmen and nice ladies from the neighborhood.

I eventually moved out west. While attending culinary school in Seattle, I stared in awe at a massive halibut's eyes, contemplating their migration from the sides of its head to the top. Two tours through Italian restaurants introduced me to the diversity of regional fish dishes. At one place I worked with tuna roe (*bottarga*), and I soaked salt cod for fritters. Lots and lots of salt cod. At the other I grilled little silver fish while the Italian owner waxed poetic about the best fish in the world (Grilled! From the Mediterranean! Salt! Olive oil! *Eccellente!*).

My most formative restaurant experience was cooking at the famous Herbfarm Restaurant in Woodinville, Washington. I was the fish girl there: I held still-quivering abalone in my hands, shucked the tiniest native Olympia oysters, faced more Dungeness crabs—antennae to eye—than I care to count, and scooped out luscious golden eggs from spiny sea urchins while wearing thick rubber gloves for self-defense. There I cradled in my arms, just barely, the stunning majesty of a forty-pound wild Alaska king salmon, as you would a precious baby, and I chuckled alongside my fellow line cooks at the phallic ridiculousness of a geoduck. I was miles and miles from the Atlantic Coast.

With the spirit of a local, I ran the galley of a boat headed up the Inside Passage to Alaska, peeling spot prawns and filleting salmon before climbing down the ladder to my quarters, each step pulling a bit more of the New Jersey out of the girl. This past winter I shed any remaining vestiges of my birthplace. I joined dozens of others on a traditional night dig for razor clams. There were cars lined up as far as the eye could see, their headlights like luminaria leading the way up the coast. When I got my limit and headed back to the cabin, I remember feeling that I had finally gone completely native.

The world of seafood is much more complicated now than it was when I pulled my first Jersey sunfish out of the lake; shortsighted economic gain, a morass of bureaucracy, and a universe of misinformation complicate it. It's clear that we have an insatiable appetite for far more than the oceans, rivers, and lakes can provide. Guilt and food are a terrible combination, certain to give you indigestion, or as my friend says, "Guilt makes for bad gravy." Denial or ignorance about the consequences of our food choices is far too widespread. Most insidious is the attitude that we might as well indulge in all types of fish while they are still around (because who knows when they might disappear).

My intention with this book is to help simplify some very complicated issues, thereby empowering you to make better, more sustainable seafood choices. There are some generally recognized sustainable seafood choices that have been vetted by the highly regarded Monterey Bay Aquarium Seafood Watch Program, among others. Many factors are considered to determine which fisheries are sustainable, including, for example, the type of gear used to harvest the fish, the relative abundance of the species, the amount of accidental bycatch of non-target species, and the safety of the waters from which the fish are harvested.

This cookbook celebrates seafood from up and down the western coast of the United States: seafood that is well managed, and fished or farmed in such a way as to protect the environment. In this book you will find recipes for seafood that is low in mercury and persistent organic pollutants (POPs), seafood that is healthful and absolutely delicious. I hope that the good management of these excellent choices and the hard work of those who educate us about making wise purchasing decisions will help keep all of these species around for a very long time.

There is a story evolving here, and the plot hinges on the health of our oceans and the sustainability of our fish. You, the consumer, are the protagonist. The most important thing you can do is ask questions. With each type of seafood I cover, I pose questions you might ask your fishmongers in order to be sure you are purchasing seafood that is healthy for you and your family as well as for our oceans. If you are satisfied with the answers, support those fishmongers. Tell your friends about them. Encourage them to continue doing the right thing by giving them your business.

Forgive me the double negative, but this book isn't about what you *shouldn't* do. It's a celebration of what you *can* do. Eat these fish with joy, share these recipes with your favorite people, and know that you are actively doing your part to ensure that seafood survives—and perhaps someday soon, thrives again.

how to use this book

This book is divided into sections based on three broad categories of seafood: shellfish (clams, mussels, oysters, Dungeness crab, shrimp, and scallops), finfish (salmon, halibut, black cod, trout, albacore tuna, and arctic char), and littlefish and eggs (sardines, squid, and caviar).

My goal is to help you feel comfortable and confident purchasing these fifteen types of sustainable seafood from your local fishmonger, fisherman, or seafood counter. Look for the following information at the beginning of each chapter:

WHAT MAKES THIS A GOOD CHOICE: Before asking you to wield your very influential buying power, I want to make sure I've given you the most current information about why I've included these particular species.

BY ANY OTHER NAME: Seafood naming can be very confusing: one person's black cod is another person's sablefish. This is the section where I list all the names you might see for the type of seafood you are purchasing. Keep in mind that the best way to identify a fish is to ask what the exact species is, which is why I have included Latin names.

SEASON: Just like produce, most types of seafood have a season; it is worth knowing so you can get the freshest quality at the right time of year. That said, well-handled frozen seafood can often be of equal or better quality than fresh. For more information, see Fresh Versus Frozen on page xxvii.

BUYING TIPS: Here is where you'll find out all the things chefs do to scope out freshness and quality in seafood.

QUESTIONS TO ASK BEFORE YOU PULL OUT YOUR WALLET: There is only so much you can see with your eyes, smell with your nose, and touch with your fingertips (before getting caught). To get all the information you want, you should have a conversation with your fishmonger or fisherman. This is a great way to find out how much or how little the person selling the seafood knows about the product. This is also the time to inquire about its origin—there is a big difference between domestic farmed shrimp and imported shrimp, for example. The more you know, the easier it will be to decide if this is the seafood you want to purchase.

CARING FOR YOUR GOOD FISH: After reading all about how to select the freshest seafood, you'll want to know how best to store it. Shellfish, finfish, littlefish, and fish eggs all have different needs. This is the section where you'll learn how to keep your seafood as fresh as possible.

HOW THIS TYPE OF SEAFOOD IS RAISED OR HARVESTED: It's incredible how often we eat things without having any idea of how they came to be. This is especially true for farmed seafood. Look to this section to learn, for example, how a mussel can be farmed or how sustainable albacore is caught.

SUSTAINABLE SUBSTITUTES: There will be times when you head out shopping with a recipe in hand looking for a specific type of seafood. It's helpful to know ahead of time what some good substitutes are in case you can't find what you're looking for, or if the quality doesn't pass muster.

Remember these "Good FISH" rules—F: Farmed can be OK (verify that it is done responsibly). I: Investigate your source (ask questions; support good chefs, fishmongers, and markets). S: Smaller is better (limit portion size; eat smaller fish, like sardines and young albacore). H: Home (buy Pacific Coast fish because the United States has higher environmental standards).

....

RECIPES

For each of the fifteen types of seafood, there are five recipes, organized from simplest to most challenging.

EASY RECIPES: The first two recipes are designed for a beginner who is eager to learn how to cook with seafood but may be intimidated by it, or the home cook who wants a recipe that can be prepared in thirty minutes or less on a weeknight. I'm a cooking teacher by profession, and I love helping novice cooks (especially intimidated novice cooks) learn how to work with seafood. In these recipes, I will gently hold your hand throughout the cooking process and hopefully anticipate any questions you might have. I tell this to all my students, but it's especially important for inexperienced cooks: make sure to read the recipe through at least twice before starting. Pay special attention to the Ingredients and Terms Defined (page xxii), Tools of the Trade (page xxiv), and Fresh Versus Frozen (page xxvii) sections as well as the Anatomy of a Flake (page 102) box. Also be sure to check out the links for online cooking videos (see How-To Videos, opposite), especially if you are a visual learner like I am.

INTERMEDIATE RECIPES: The next two recipes are written for a more experienced home cook; these recipes can be prepared in under an hour. These medium-level recipes also expose you to less familiar species (geoduck) and ingredients (shiso, kombu, hijiki), and they may require some special equipment (a wok or ice cream machine) and advanced prep time (presalting or marinating fish).

ADVANCED RECIPES: The last recipe of the five is designed for the adventurous and involved cook, perhaps a self-described "weekend warrior"—someone who is happy spending several hours in the kitchen and likes a challenge. It is also meant to appeal to my fellow chefs out there who want to flip directly to recipes that involve more advanced techniques such as fish smoking, pasta making, curing, or working with multiple steps, components, and/or garnishes.

WINE PAIRINGS: Wine pairings are selected by my partner in life, work, and sometimes crime, the lovely (no bias here) and talented sommelier April Pogue. April has worked at some of the finest restaurants on the West Coast: Fifth Floor in San Francisco, Spago Beverly Hills, and in Seattle at Earth & Ocean (in the W Hotel), Yarrow Bay Grill, and Wild Ginger.

HOW-TO VIDEOS

Scattered throughout the book are links to short, fun how-to videos (denoted with the symbol ‡) in which I show you how to perform some techniques that are hard to capture in words. Check out www.goodfishbook.com, where you'll see the following:

- *How to select quality seafood*
- *How to clean a geoduck*
- *How to debeard, clean, and store mussels*
- *How to shuck an oyster*
- *How to cook and clean a Dungeness crab*
- *How to devein shrimp*
- *How to sear a scallop*
- *How to remove the skin from a fish fillet*
- *How to remove pin bones from salmon, trout, or char*
- *How to fillet a fish*
- *How to wok-smoke fish*
- *How to debone a whole trout for stuffing*
- *How to butterfly and debone a sardine*
- *How to clean and cut up a whole squid*
- *How to make a quenelle with caviar*

April first gives you her ideal pairing—a varietal she hopes you'll be able to find at your local wine shop—listing a specific bottle she tasted with the dish and declared to be a great match. If you aren't able to find her first choice, she offers a secondary varietal as a good alternative. From time to time I butt my nose in and offer you a booze or beer pairing.

INGREDIENTS AND TERMS DEFINED

CLAM JUICE: If you don't have extra seafood stock stored in your freezer, bottled or canned clam juice makes a flavorful stock. Be sure to season your recipe cautiously as different brands can vary in saltiness.

DICING: *Small dice:* Technically—as in "culinary school instructor walking around class with a ruler"—this is defined as ¼ inch by ¼ inch by ¼ inch, but just use that as a very rough guide. *Medium dice:* ½ inch by ½ inch by ½ inch. *Large dice:* ¾ inch by ¾ inch by ¾ inch.

DRY WHITE VERMOUTH: We're mostly red wine drinkers in my house, and I used to feel guilty cooking with white wine and then later realizing it had gone bad before we remembered to drink it. Dry white vermouth has a long shelf life and tastes delicious when used as a cooking wine—after all, it's a fortified white wine infused with herbs and spices. (I thank my friend Susan for teaching me this handy tip.)

FISH SAUCE: Fish sauce can be found in the Asian foods aisle of large supermarkets. It's made from fermented anchovies or shrimp and is one of those very special ingredients that adds an incredible salty-savory flavor to foods. One wonders who the first person was to taste the fermented juices of rotting anchovies and declare it a delicious seasoning, but incredibly, they were right. Fish sauce on its own is pungent; in a dish it is magical. I've used many brands throughout the years with good results, but Tiparos and Squid Brand are high quality, and I usually have both on hand. There's no need to refrigerate fish sauce: it's already rotten!

HIGH-HEAT VEGETABLE OIL: A lot of folks don't know that each type of oil has a different point at which it will start smoking/burning (called the smoke point) and that smoking oils can be carcinogenic. I like to teach people to use the right oil for the job. When I specify using a high-heat vegetable oil for sautéing, panfrying, or stir-frying, use any of the following oils: peanut, safflower, sunflower, coconut, or grapeseed. You can also fry with clarified butter (ghee). Look for expeller-pressed oils that are mechanically, not chemically, refined.

JERSEY GIRL: See Introduction (page xvii). Exit 28, in case you're wondering.

LEMON JUICE: Always fresh squeezed, pretty please.

MIRIN: Mirin is a sweet rice wine that can be found in the Asian foods aisle of most large supermarkets. Substitute with two parts sake to one part sugar, or in a pinch, two parts dry white wine to one part sugar.

PACIFIC COAST: For the purposes of this book, I've selected seafood that is either native to or farmed from California up the coast through Canada and into Alaska.

PANKO: Panko is a flaked Japanese bread crumb that is becoming more and more popular as a substitute for old-fashioned bread crumbs. I really like the texture it lends to pan-fried foods, especially oysters or fried fillets—it seems to give the food an extra lightness and crunchiness. I know it has hit the mainstream because out on Washington's Long Beach Peninsula—which is razor-clamming territory—I saw it being sold in a large bulk bin at the local supermarket/hardware store.

SAKE: Sake can now be found at most large supermarkets where wine is sold; you can substitute Chinese rice wine.

SALT: For the purposes of this book, unless otherwise specified, assume sea salt. If you prefer to use kosher salt, double the amount (kosher salt takes up more volume with its larger crystals), but as always, season to taste. If you're using Morton iodized salt, I have no comment. No, that's not true, I do have a comment: Have you tasted it recently? On its own? It tastes terrible!

SEASONED RICE WINE VINEGAR: I use this ingredient a lot throughout the book. This is a convenience product made of rice vinegar that has some salt and sugar in it. If you have plain rice wine vinegar, just lightly heat it and dissolve some salt and sugar in it to taste. Seasoned rice wine vinegar makes the simplest dressing ever: just toss it with cucumbers, carrots, sesame seeds, etcetera—no oil necessary.

SHISO: Shiso (also known as *perilla*) is sometimes called Japanese mint. You can find it at Japanese or Asian markets. Substitute with spearmint.

TAMARIND: Tamarind is sold in several forms: dried in the pod (in the produce section of some stores, especially Mexican markets); as a paste, with or without seeds; and as a thin concentrate. To remove seeds and sticky pulp, rehydrate the paste or pod innards in a small amount of hot water, then push the tamarind through a sieve. For use in recipes, one teaspoon paste is the equivalent of one tablespoon concentrate. Tamarind—in one form or another—is becoming very easy to find these days, but if you're having difficulty, lemon juice works fine in a pinch.

TOOLS OF THE TRADE

CAST-IRON SKILLET: I love cast iron so much, I wrote a dorky poem about it.

ODE TO A CAST-IRON SKILLET

Carry that weight and think of your foremothers
Who never needed gym memberships—if they
could even imagine them.
Heave that iron and fight osteoporosis; your skillet
is a healer, a weapon, and a tool.

Only in modern times could we cast aside cast iron
In favor of flimsy fry pans with deeply etched scars.
Heft that pan! Sear that scallop! Bake that cornbread!

Carry that weight and think of your foremothers
Who never had those little flaps of skin under their arms.

FILLETING KNIFE (1 AND 8): Your knife need not be expensive or fancy, but it should be ever so slightly flexible to help you maneuver around delicate, curved rib bones. I think one in the range of seven inches is good for working with both small and larger fish. I like to use a larger knife (1), sometimes called a scimitar knife, to fillet whole salmon or albacore.

FISH SCALER (3): Like pin boning, fish scaling is a job that fishmongers are happy to do for you, and for many reasons, you should be happy they are happy to do it. It's a messy job, and I know from experience that despite submerging the fish in a sink of cold water (highly encouraged), those scales tend to go everywhere, including onto your skin, where they become one with you. However, you might find yourself needing to scale a fish that was caught by someone you know, in which case this nifty tool will come in handy. Place the fish in a sink of cold water, wear an apron, and then run this tool from tail to head, grabbing and pulling off the scales. You can use a spoon if you don't have a fish scaler handy (not as effective, but still workable).

FISH SPATULA (7): Sometimes it all comes down to the right tool—and a fish spatula, with its thin, metal, slightly upturned edge, really helps gently flip or transfer a delicate fillet or whole fish.

FISH TWEEZERS (6): Fishmongers are usually happy to remove pin bones from salmon, trout, or char if you ask nicely, but sometimes they don't take enough care and can snap them in half or tear the flesh. The pin bones that run through a salmon or trout fillet can be brittle, and it takes some finesse to remove them (go to www.goodfishbook.com to watch me demonstrate the technique). If you decide you want to try it yourself, you'll need a pair of fish tweezers. In a pinch, I've used clean needle-nose pliers (5) or even kitchen tongs to remove pin bones.

LABRADOR RETRIEVER: Feel free to substitute another breed or any mutt. Nothing is more effective at cleaning a kitchen floor than a dog. Ours is a canine Zamboni, efficiently wet-mopping our floor with her tongue just as soon as we say the word.

OYSTER SHUCKER (4): I've seen cooks and deckhands, fishermen and drunks open oysters with all manner of things: knives, screwdrivers, a hammer and nail, and keys. Just because it can be done doesn't mean it *should* be done, especially if you are a beginner. Whether your shucker is blunt or sharp is a personal choice, though I recommend blunt if you are a novice. Go to www.goodfishbook.com for a demonstration of how to shuck oysters.

SCRUB BRUSH (2): A solid, stiff brush will come in handy when I suggest scrubbing off the little barnacle bits that have jumped on board your oyster shell, or the fibrous strands of algae and whatnot on your mussels. Wild clams, too, can use a good scrubbing.

SPICE GRINDER: Also known as a coffee grinder, but don't make the mistake of using your dedicated coffee grinder for grinding spices unless the sound of cumin- or turmeric-infused coffee appeals to you. I keep a separate grinder just for spices. I also put a piece of blue painter's tape around the outside with the word "spices" scrawled on it so April doesn't sleepily confuse it with the coffee grinder.

I find a spice grinder to be an indispensable kitchen tool. You know those fancy, expensive spice blends that all the chefs are marketing these days? Some fresh spices plus a spice grinder plus two minutes is all that keeps you from creating your own fresh blends with which to dress that gorgeous piece of fish before throwing it on the grill. I provide several recipes for spice blends that will get you started.

sustainable seafood basics

FRESH VERSUS FROZEN

Ah, that age-old question for which too many have a knee-jerk answer: "Oh," they say, "I only buy my fish fresh, never frozen!"

Not all fresh fish are the same, and you may be shocked to know that "fresh" does not have any legally defined meaning. A fish that has never been frozen but is eleven days past harvest, was poorly handled, and is in questionable condition can still be marketed and sold as fresh. Alternatively, a well-handled fresh fish (and by "well-handled" I mean landed gently, bled, and quickly chilled) has a longer shelf life, and its quality can be maintained for many days out of the water. A quality fresh fish will have its scales intact and will smell good; its flesh will be firm enough that a touch to its skin will not leave an impression. (Go to www.goodfishbook.com for a demonstration of how to select quality seafood.)

Not all frozen fish are the same. Again, it comes down to the handling. A well-handled fish prior to freezing makes all the difference in the world. Many fish are frozen right at sea and can be extremely high quality. Alternatively, if a fish is banged around and not chilled down quickly enough, the frozen product will

HOW TO SAFELY THAW FROZEN FISH

The best way to thaw a frozen piece of fish is to leave it overnight in the fridge. If you are in a pinch and need it quickly, put the fillet in a resealable plastic bag inside a large metal bowl filled with cold water. Replace the water with fresh cold water every half hour, until the fillet is thawed. Why not use warm water to speed up the process? Two reasons: 1. Warm water—depending on how warm—could actually start to cook the delicate fillet. 2. Thawing is safest out of the "danger zone," which is 40° to 140°F. Thawing with warm water would put the fish in perfect bacterial heaven: great for the bacteria, not so much for you. Keep it cold.

A PROPERLY FROZEN FISH

Sustainable seafood educator Amy Grondin (also a commercial fisherman) helped simplify for me the commercial freezing process that brings high-quality frozen fish to our markets. I'll let her explain in her own words:

"To maintain the quality of fish as a frozen product, fish must be frozen to below 0°F/–18°C as quickly as possible. Fish tissue can contain up to 80 percent water and has little connective tissue to hold the cells together. When water freezes, it expands. If the freezing happens quickly, the ice crystals formed in the fish are small and cause minimal change to the cell structure of the flesh. When the fish is slowly defrosted in a refrigerator in a drip pan, the result is a firm piece of fish.

"Freezing fish slowly makes big ice crystals that break the connective tissue and cell walls of the fish. The fish will be mushy when it is defrosted. Think of the bottle you accidentally left in the freezer when attempting a quick chill. The same thing happens to the fish flesh when you try to freeze it at home.

"The freezers used on fishing boats and by processors are not the same as a domestic freezer, which is designed to hold frozen products, not create them. Industrial freezers use blast units and other techniques that freeze fish quickly, bringing the fish through the critical temperature zone between 32°F/0°C and 0°F/–18°C where cell damage can occur."

suffer: the telltale signs will be water loss, gaping, and tearing. Home freezers are not designed to freeze fish well, but, that said, I've had success with really good, well-handled albacore tuna loins I've vacuum-sealed them, frozen them, and then used them within two months.

If you don't live near a local source of fish, there is a carbon-footprint benefit to purchasing your fish frozen. Fresh fish needs to be flown all over the world, consuming huge quantities of jet fuel in order to get to you, whereas frozen fish can be delivered via more fuel-efficient means, such as ship, rail, or truck.

FARMED VERSUS WILD

Which is better? I'd like to tell you that there is a very simple answer to this question, but the fact remains that the answer is: it depends. Half the people I talk to assume that farmed fish is bad and wild is good. The other half think we need to stop eating all wild fish to give them a break and eat only farmed fish. My goal here is to simplify the issue as much as humanly possible without glossing over some important points. That's a hard task, but work with me through this overview.

Wild Fish

Many species of wild fish are doing quite well. Their fisheries are well managed, which means that the catch is highly regulated, preserving fish for future generations. Furthermore, the environment is not destroyed in the process of catching these fish. Pacific Coast albacore and the five species of Alaska wild salmon come to mind. Pacific Coast squid don't seem to be threatened. Ditto for wild sardines.

What's important to keep in mind when purchasing wild fish is how they were caught. The most environmentally sound way to catch fish is in small, focused quantities. Examples include "trolling"—also known as "hook and line"—which is essentially the commercial version of dipping a fishing pole into the ocean; catching shrimp or crabs in a pot; and small-scale purse seining (using a net to enclose a school of fish).

Other methods are not as ocean- and fish-friendly. Two big ones I try to avoid are fish caught by dredging/trawling (which, unfortunately, sounds very similar to "trolling") and certain kinds of long-lining. Trawling scrapes the ocean floor by dragging heavy weighted nets, which is especially bad if there is sensitive habitat there (very often the case). Trawling also produces a lot of "bycatch." Bycatch consists of nontargeted, accidentally caught species, which are often unintentionally killed in the fishing process. Not only is this a complete waste of protein, if the bycatch includes juvenile fish killed before they can spawn, it upsets the life cycle of the species. Bycatch is bad all around, and it's crucial that commercial fisheries limit it as much as possible.

Long-lining involves dragging lots of lines, armed with many hooks that drop down at regular intervals, often for miles on end. It is most problematic when fisheries use it to catch fish in the top part of the ocean column, because the line sits on the surface, and all sorts of unintended species get hooked (turtles, birds, etc.). After so much time on the line, many of these animals are dead when it is finally hauled in. Bycatch, therefore, is also a rampant problem with

> *The important questions to ask* when buying wild fish are: what is the species, where was it caught, and how was it caught? If you want Pacific Coast wild seafood, you can feel good picking the types I specify in this book, though keep in mind that this is a constantly evolving story—which makes a resource like Monterey Bay Aquarium's Seafood Watch indispensable (see page 239 for contact information).

this type of fishing. Luckily, not all long-lining is the same, and there are major exceptions: long-lining along the bottom of the ocean—for example, in Alaska's sustainable halibut and black cod fisheries—has a much better track record of catching only intended species.

Farmed Fish

Let's clear up a common misconception: while there can be some issues with shellfish farming (obstructed access to beaches, complaints of unsightliness, litter), in general it is extremely sustainable for two very important reasons. First, farmed shellfish are not fed using wild fish feed, so there is no negative drawing of species (protein loss) from the oceans to convert to feed. Second, farmed shellfish, just like wild shellfish, filter feed, thus contributing to better water quality. There are few simple decisions when it comes to eating seafood ethically, but here is one: shellfish such as oysters, clams, and mussels make the oceans cleaner. Three cheers for these little pumping filter feeders!

Let's move on to fish farming. On the Pacific Coast we're mainly talking about salmon farms, which are located right on the ocean's shores (versus on land in a closed-containment system). This method of farming carries with it huge problems. Studies are finding that ocean farming hurts wild fish. Think of it this way: if there were an outbreak of disease on an island where there were no ferries or bridges, the disease would be self-limiting. Compare this to a disease breaking out in the middle of New York City—pretty limitless how far that disease could spread, right? It just seems like a bad idea to mix and mingle high-density fish farms right in the middle of wild-fish ocean migration routes. The ocean is an extremely efficient distribution medium; we need to be very careful about what we introduce into this vast open system. Closed-containment land-based farms make a lot more sense.

Other issues worth considering when thinking about fish farming are feed ratio and quality of feed. Carnivorous fish at the top of the food chain require a lot of wild fish feed to convert to usable protein. (For example, farmed bluefin tuna are said to have a feed ratio of anywhere from 5:1 all the way up to 20:1—depending on how big the fish and which study you're looking at—where the first number is pounds of wild feed to produce the second number, pounds of fish flesh.) It is much more sustainable to choose fish lower on the food chain that are either vegetarian or require small amounts of fish protein to produce their flesh. Another issue worth exploring is the quality of the feed given to farmed fish. I'm interested in the sustainability of our oceans but also in the health of the fish for those who consume it. Farmed fish may be a renewable resource, but if that fish is fed genetically modified grains treated with chemicals, I can't, in good conscience, get behind it. This is an area that needs more investigation; consumer pressure will help get to the bottom of these issues.

LESS IS MORE

We humans eat too much fish.

We humans eat too much of the same kinds of fish.

Farmed salmon, imported farmed shrimp, and wild fish, such as bluefin tuna, are in such high demand that they are produced or harvested in staggering, unbelievable numbers. In the case of offshore farming, the fish are packed into cages like sardines in a can, escape into wild populations, spread disease, and create all sorts of problems for our environment. Antibiotics are applied en masse by many offshore farming operations to control outbreaks of disease; unfortunately, those diseases, not to mention the antibiotics, still find a way to get into our oceans. In the case of bluefin tuna (and other wild species), we are simply fishing them into extinction.

We humans have forgotten that fish have a season, just like produce. We have forgotten that there is a cost associated with getting what we want whenever we want it. Generally speaking, industrial fishing operations have become too damn good at catching wild fish—at any cost—and too greedy and shortsighted when it comes to farming them. At this rate, we will eat all the wild fish and destroy the environment farming finfish in offshore farms. An industrial model of fishing, just like farming or meat production, is incredibly efficient on the one hand and incredibly destructive on the other. Closed-containment land-based fish farming (versus offshore open-net farming), shellfish farming, and a local fishery model hold the potential to address some of our biggest concerns,

THREE CHOICES CAN MAKE A WORLD OF DIFFERENCE

1. *Diversify the kinds of fish you eat.* There are five species of salmon, not just king and sockeye. Little silver fish such as sardines and anchovies are delicious, nutritious, and affordable.

2. *Be selective with your seafood purchases.* We have a lot of power as consumers. Pull out your wallet only when you are comfortable that the fish you have selected is both healthy for you and for the planet. You deserve to eat high-quality fish. Future generations also deserve to have what you have.

3. *Limit the amount of seafood on your plate.* I've written my recipes to reflect my desire to rearrange the priorities on our plates. Generally speaking, ¼ pound of seafood per person is affordable and reasonable (for shellfish I recommend about ½ pound per person to account for the weight of the shells). Most of my recipes are based on a meal for four, so I recommend buying 1 pound of quality sustainable seafood. It's budget friendly and planet friendly. We're all supposed to be eating more vegetables anyway, so let this cookbook give you a gentle push in that direction. Less is more.

although these systems are not perfect. At this point, though, perfect should not be the enemy of good.

We humans need to think about fish and fishermen the way we have started to think about produce and farmers: the closer you are to your food source, the better your ability to know what you are eating.

SHELLFISH

— clams —

New Jersey: August 1978. I can still smell the scent of hundreds of clams splitting themselves open in our speckled and spigoted black-and-white steamer pot. Our family lived in three houses on the lake, separated by one mile and the time it took for short legs to traverse the distance. Each house presented a different snack opportunity, with my aunt and uncle's place being the dinnertime final destination. On late summer days we would gather there, sunburned and boat-weary, and circle a large pot, filled to the rim with more clams than we believed the pot should hold.

These clams were my very first taste of shellfish, and it's true what they say: you always remember your first. Their bounce-back brininess—their sweetness and salinity—formed the centerpiece of so many of our summers. Clams, shared with my boisterous and loving family, etched themselves firmly onto my culinary map. They were my proverbial first dip of the toe into the ocean. I was hooked early, at age 8, and my familial clan of shellfish worshippers could only clutch helplessly at their wallets because lobster was just around the next corner.

HOW THIS TYPE OF SEAFOOD IS RAISED OR HARVESTED: In commercial clam farming, clam "seed" are collected in the wild or in hatcheries, then commonly transferred as juveniles for what's known as "grow-out" on the seafloor. Clams are placed either directly on the seafloor or in nets, bags, or trays. They need to be able to burrow. Most Pacific Coast clams are harvested with hand rakes. Farmed geoducks are harvested by divers (at high tide) with the use of pressurized high-volume water guns. Razor clams are harvested by hand, using either a shovel or a "clam gun."

SUSTAINABLE SUBSTITUTES: In most recipes, it is fairly easy to substitute one type of shellfish for another. If fresh clams are not available, look for mussels. Another option would be to use frozen razor clams.

All commercial shellfish come with harvest tags that list the date and location from which the shellfish were taken. If you ask someone to produce this tag and they can't, turn on your heel and make a dramatic exit (with lots of flair) because they have not earned your business. Shellfish of dubious origin is not to be trusted.

steamers with beer

Back in the day, my family would get wild clams from Asbury Park on the Jersey shore. We preferred littlenecks or cherrystones and believed the smallest clams were the most desirable (which gave us something to fight over). Here on the Pacific Coast, it's manila and native littleneck country. If you have someone in your family who is a bivalve-a-phobe, this is the perfect gateway recipe. We used St. Pauli Girl, but any light beer will do.

SERVES A ROWDY FAMILY OF 6 TO 8

2 cans beer

2 onions, cut into medium dice

3 ribs celery, sliced ¼ inch thin

1 tablespoon Old Bay seasoning

5 pounds clams, scrubbed

1 cup (2 sticks) unsalted butter, melted, foam skimmed

1 cup cocktail sauce (make your own by combining ½ cup ketchup and ½ cup prepared horseradish with lemon juice and salt to taste)

4 lemons, cut into wedges

In a large steamer pot (or you could use a pasta pot and steam the clams in two batches), combine the beer, onions, celery, and Old Bay seasoning. Let the liquid come to a boil and then reduce the heat and simmer for 5 minutes before adding the clams (in the steaming basket) on top. Cover the pot. As the clams start to open (check after 3 to 4 minutes), start removing them with tongs to a heated bowl. (Any clams that do not open can be pried open using an oyster shucker or discarded.)

Serve the clams with bowls of melted butter, cocktail sauce, lemon wedges, and tiny cocktail forks. You can also dip the clams into the steaming brew. If you're really fond of salt, beer, and clams, you'll want to do what my grandfather did: use the spigot on the bottom of the steamer pot and pour yourself a mug of the infused brew. "Papa" wasn't a drinking man, but he sure liked his salty clam brew.

PAIRING: Beer! And make it cheap.

geoduck crudo with shiso oil

Random geoduck factoid: The oldest geoduck lived for 164 years. Let's take a moment to appreciate that. Somehow, this rather vulnerable clam, with the majority of its body outside of its protective shell, eluded predators and survived for a century and a half buried deep in the soft sand. Pretty incredible. Not-so-random geoduck factoid: No one—and I mean absolutely no one—*can hold a geoduck and resist giggling.*

SERVES 4 AS AN APPETIZER

½ pound geoduck siphon meat, well cleaned‡

½ cup extra-virgin olive oil

1 tablespoon seasoned rice wine vinegar

6 fresh shiso leaves

Freshly ground pink peppercorns

Gray sea salt

Slice the geoduck paper thin with a very sharp knife and keep it cold in the refrigerator while you prepare the garnishes.

Combine the olive oil and rice wine vinegar with the shiso in a blender or food processor, and blend into a smooth, light green emulsion. Transfer the shiso oil to a squeeze bottle or a small jar with a narrow opening (you will have some left over: refrigerate it and use it on salads).

Place the geoduck slices decoratively on a platter, each slice slightly overlapping the previous one. Generously drizzle the shiso oil over the top. Season to taste with pink peppercorns and sea salt.

‡ Go to www.goodfishbook.com for a demonstration of how to clean a geoduck.

PAIRING: Junmai-shu sake or a northern Rhône white.

Rolling the dough: Using a hand-cranked pasta machine, divide the dough into 2 workable pieces (keep one wrapped while you roll out the other). Run each piece through the machine on setting #1 (the widest setting on your machine). Fold it into three pieces (like a letter), and run it through again, inserting the narrow end first. Set the machine to setting #2 and repeat the process, dusting with flour as necessary. At this point, you don't need to fold the dough. Keep running it through each setting down to #6 or #7, depending on how thin you want the dough. I think a thinner noodle works well for this recipe.

Partially drying the pasta sheets: I like to lay the pasta sheets on a lightly floured counter for 10 minutes or so, flipping them over after 5 minutes. This dries them slightly, which is a good thing at this stage, as it will keep the individual noodles from sticking to each other when you cut the dough. Next, run the pasta sheets through the fettuccine cutter attachment on your pasta machine. Dust the noodles with flour and keep them spread out on the counter until you are ready to boil them. If you want to freeze them, wait about 30 more minutes, until they have dried further, and pull the pasta together into several bundles. Freeze these on a sheet pan, then transfer them to a resealable plastic freezer bag. Use within 2 weeks. You can cook the pasta directly from the freezer; just add a minute or so to the cooking time.

— mussels —

Shelton, Washington: January 2010. Gordon King, masterful mussel man and walking font of shellfish knowledge, whisks us out to the mussel rafts at Taylor Shellfish Farms. It's cold and windy and we're bundled up—hats, down coats, gloves, scarves. Gordon (in shorts) jumps out of the skiff and up onto the narrow, grated edging of the raft and shows us the lines where farmed mussels stretch far down into the water, filter feeding and thinking their mussel-y thoughts (which I imagine are quite limited).

Gordon is as passionate about farming mussels as I am about preparing them. The process is more straightforward than I had imagined it would be. Larvae are grown in a hatchery, placed onto mesh socks, dropped into Puget Sound, and then one-and-a-half years later are harvested by hand and sent to the processing plant where they are separated and cleaned.

First we are shown the adult mussels—ready to be harvested later that day. Moments later Gordon pulls up a rope gripped tightly by black-brown adolescents. Then he moves on to the other raft where the little babies, no bigger than a pinkie nail, are being lowered into their socks to take up residence for a time.

I draw my scarf tightly around my neck and turn away from the wind while scribbling notes in a little book. Later that night, a five-pound bag of mussels in the backseat, I stop by the market and pull out my note. It says: Mussels. Bread. Guinness. Cream. *Test this.*

mussels with guinness cream

2 pounds mussels

1 tablespoon extra-virgin olive oil

¼ cup minced shallots

Pinch of salt

⅛ teaspoon cayenne

¾ cup Guinness extra stout

¾ cup cream

1 teaspoon freshly grated or prepared horseradish

1 teaspoon honey

2 tablespoons unsalted butter

2 tablespoons minced fresh Italian parsley

Good, crusty bread

I try to eat fairly lightly, and that means I don't reach for cream every time I cook. Cream is a wonderful thing, but it can also be a crutch masking the flavors of the food it is paired with rather than elevating them. I tend to use cream judiciously, with the precision of a rifle, saving the cream cannon for ice cream. Then, one day, while developing mussel recipes, I hit on a major exception to this rule. It was on this auspicious day that Cream met Guinness, and a romance was born. Guinness elevated Cream into a decadent, malty, richer version of itself, and Cream elevated Guinness by rounding its caramel and chocolate edge with a warm white blanket. They lived happily ever after.

SERVES 4 AS A LIGHT DINNER

Scrub and debeard the mussels.‡

Heat a large pot over medium-high heat. Add the olive oil; when it is hot, add the shallots and salt. Sauté for 5 minutes, or until the shallots are lightly browned. Add the cayenne, Guinness, cream, horseradish, honey, and mussels. Toss the mussels, coating them with the sauce. Cover the pot, turn the heat to high, and cook for 3 minutes. Stir the mussels, and when most of them have opened, transfer them with a slotted spoon to a large serving bowl. (Any mussels that do not open can be pried open using an oyster shucker or discarded.) Boil the sauce gently until reduced by half. Turn off the heat, swirl in the butter and parsley, taste for seasoning, and pour the sauce over the mussels. Serve with bread to dip in the Guinness cream.

‡ Go to www.goodfishbook.com for a demonstration of how to debeard and clean mussels.

PAIRING: Guinness beer, but of course.

mussels with apple cider and thyme glaze

It seems that most mussel recipes fall into two camps. The first camp has mussels mingling with garlic, tomatoes, parsley, and white wine. It's a nice camp: familiar, warm, and predictable. The second camp is more exotic, and there is where you'll find mussels dipped into a curry broth of coconut milk and chilies. I like both camps. I've been to them, many times. But I'd like to take you to a different camp—a camp where mussels hang out with mustard and thyme and apple cider. I think you'll like it here.

SERVES 4 AS A LIGHT DINNER

....

Scrub and debeard the mussels.‡

Add the hard apple cider and thyme sprigs to a pot over high heat. Add the mussels, cover, and cook for about 3 minutes, or until the mussels open. (Any mussels that do not open can be pried open using an oyster shucker or discarded.) Transfer the mussels to a large heatproof bowl, and cover to keep warm. Strain the mussel liquor through a fine mesh sieve and set aside.

Melt the butter in a small saucepan over medium-low heat. Stir in the shallots and cook for about 1 minute, or until they are fragrant. Add the reserved mussel liquor, apple cider, apple cider vinegar, and clam juice. Cook until the sauce is reduced by three quarters, about 20 minutes. Remove from the heat and stir in the mustard, chopped thyme, and capers. Season to taste with salt and pepper and pour the sauce over the mussels.

‡ Go to www.goodfishbook.com for a demonstration of how to debeard and clean mussels.

PAIRING: A Savennières, such as Domaine Jo Pithon "La Croix Picot" 2008, Loire Valley, France, or an Alsatian pinot gris.

2 pounds mussels

¼ cup hard apple cider, such as Hornsby's

2 sprigs fresh thyme, plus 1 teaspoon chopped fresh thyme

1 tablespoon unsalted butter

3 tablespoons minced shallots

¾ cup apple or pear cider

1 teaspoon apple cider vinegar

¼ cup clam juice

1 tablespoon grainy Dijon mustard

1 teaspoon chopped capers

Salt and freshly ground pepper

mussels with pancetta and vermouth

My friend Ashlyn introduced me to a version of this recipe. She grew up in Louisiana and Mississippi and loved eating Oysters Bienville, a famous dish from New Orleans, which she then adapted by replacing the original seafood with mussels. In honor of Ashlyn, I'd like to tell you her favorite one-liner that she says every single time I mention I'm cooking mussels (or clams, or oysters, for that matter): "Vanna," she says, "I'd like to bivalve."

SERVES 6 TO 8 AS AN APPETIZER

2 pounds mussels

¼ cup dry white vermouth or dry white wine

2 ounces pancetta, prosciutto, or bacon

¼ cup finely minced shallots

Zest of 1 lemon (about 2 teaspoons), plus lemon juice for finishing

¼ teaspoon cayenne

2 tablespoons mayonnaise

2 tablespoons minced fresh Italian parsley

¼ cup panko or bread crumbs

2 ounces (½ cup) grated Manchego cheese

Rock salt, for serving

Scrub and debeard the mussels.‡

Preheat the broiler. Place a rack in the lower middle position of the oven.

Put the mussels and vermouth in a saucepan over high heat and cover. Cook just until the mussels pop open, 2 to 3 minutes. Remove them with tongs as they open. (Any mussels that do not open can be pried open using an oyster shucker or discarded.) When the mussels are done, strain the mussel liquor and reserve. Let the mussels cool.

In a wide sauté pan, cook the pancetta over medium heat until it releases some of its fat, about 5 minutes. Add the shallots and cook, stirring occasionally, until they are soft, about 5 more minutes. Add the reserved mussel liquor, lemon zest, and cayenne and deglaze the pan, letting the juices evaporate completely. Transfer the mixture to a bowl and fold in the mayonnaise. In a separate bowl, mix the parsley and panko.

When the mussels are cool, twist off the top shells and discard. Place the mussels in their bottom shells on a sheet pan. Top each mussel with a small amount of the pancetta-shallot mixture and then coat the top with some of the parsley-panko mixture. Finish each with a sprinkle of Manchego.

(continued)

to a large bowl, removing and discarding their shells, and set aside. Strain the mussel liquor through a fine mesh sieve and add ½ cup of the liquor to the cabbage. Discard the rest or use it in a soup or sauce the next night.

Dredge the mussels in the flour and shake them in a strainer to remove any excess. In a large sauté pan over high heat, add the vegetable oil. When it is hot, sear the mussels until caramelized on both sides, about 4 minutes total.

To serve, pile the mussels on top of the warm cabbage and serve with a bowl of aioli on the side for dipping.

* Piment d'Espelette can be found in Spanish or French specialty stores or through online sources.

‡ Go to www.goodfishbook.com for a demonstration of how to debeard and clean mussels.

PAIRING: An albariño, such as Adegas Gran Vinum Esencia Divina Albariño 2008, Rías Baixas, Spain, or a grenache-based Spanish rosé.

— oysters —

I remember eating my first raw oyster just as surely as others remember their first lake dive, hands pointed together in prayer, toes death-gripped to the splintery edge of the dock. Truth be told, my experience was a culinary half step. I couldn't quite get myself to tackle the whole oyster, so I licked shyly at the liquor. Surprised at how delicious it was, I then drank it with gusto, letting my friend eat the oyster itself, while she puzzled at my strange workaround. When I finally went whole hog a few months later and tipped the entire oyster back, I realized all that fear and trepidation were for naught.

A little fear before trying something new is to be expected; but surely it is the wise who know that working through that fear as quickly as possible can lead to a lifetime of culinary enjoyment. For those still perched on the dock's edge: fried oysters are a damn fine baby step.

WHAT MAKES THIS A GOOD CHOICE: Whether they are wild or farmed, oysters act as filter feeders, improving ocean water quality. Like all shellfish, their needs are simple: they eat solely from the phytoplankton floating by (no wild fish meal required). Oysters are healthful: they are high in vitamin B_{12}, iron, and calcium; one oyster contains 370 mg of omega-3 fatty acids.

....

BY ANY OTHER NAME: There are five species of oysters commonly found on the Pacific Coast:

Pacific oysters (*Crassostrea giga*) were brought to the Pacific Coast from Japan in the 1920s. Most Pacific oysters (as well as Eastern oysters) are named for the bay or inlet where they are grown rather than the species. For example, California's Tomales Bay or Drakes Bay oysters both happen to be Pacific oysters (ditto for Canada's Fanny Bay oysters), so it gets sort of confusing. Like all oysters, their flavor changes depending on where they grow. This is the ultimate pleasure of being an oyster aficionado—like wine, oysters have *terroir*. Pacific varieties can get really, really big (which, in my opinion, makes for better barbecue or chowder).

Olympia oysters (*Ostrea conchaphila* or *O. lurida*), aka Olys, are the tiniest and most celebrated oysters on the Pacific Coast, and also our only native species. Olys were so popular during the gold rush that they were nearly eradicated; back in the mid-1850s, single Olympia oysters went for a silver dollar, the equivalent of about $25 per oyster today. Olympias are a great starter for a raw-oyster newbie—they're so small, they're cute, and it's hard to be intimidated by cute.

Kumamoto oysters (*Crassostrea sikamea*), aka Kumos, are appreciated by all for their sweetness; their beautiful deep, sculptured shell; and the fact that they are still at their best into the summer, when other oysters diminish in quality due to spawning. They are often described as sweet, creamy, and nutty, and are also a great first oyster for half-shell virgins.

Eastern oysters (*Crassostrea virginica*), aka Virginicas, Gulf oysters, or American oysters, are truly American, ranging up and down the East Coast, along the Gulf of Mexico, and also here on the Pacific Coast. They tend to be firmer when grown in colder northern climes, which makes for a delicious oyster on the half shell. A Totten Inlet Virginica I had in Washington tasted of the sea, with a finish that lasted forever, like the very best kind of wine.

European flats (*Ostrea edulis*), aka Belons, were introduced to the Northwest in the 1950s and, not surprisingly, are native to Europe. Like the related Olympia oyster, the parent holds on to the developing larvae within the shell before releasing it into the water after a few weeks. European flats are round in shape with an extremely shallow cup. The shells are quite brittle, and the oysters are very briny.

....

SEASON: The rule "Only eat oysters in months with an 'r' in them" (so, for example, don't eat oysters in May, June, July, or August) is sort of right, sort of not. I don't eat oysters when they spawn (reproduce), which is usually during the hotter months. An August oyster might be watery, gritty, and lacking in flavor. Generally speaking, oysters are better in the colder months, but modern refrigeration makes the rule less accurate. A nonspawning oyster harvested in the summer that is well handled can be delicious.

....

BUYING TIPS: You'll find live oysters either in saltwater tanks or stored on ice. As with all shellfish, you'll want to buy them live. You won't find oysters, unlike clams or mussels, slightly open. Or rather, if you find an oyster slightly open, it's probably dead. Oysters know how delicious they are—it's easier to get into Fort Knox than it is to get into a really fresh oyster.

....

QUESTIONS TO ASK BEFORE YOU PULL OUT YOUR WALLET: Ask to see the harvest tag so you know when the oysters were pulled out of the water. They can have a shelf life of up to two weeks, but when eating them raw, I prefer to get oysters that are as fresh as possible. I feel they taste best when I'm standing knee-deep in the water, shucking the oyster against my thigh and eating it right there. I think the quality and flavor lessens the longer and farther away you are from this idyllic picture.

....

CARING FOR YOUR GOOD FISH: You'll commonly find fresh oysters in two forms: in their shell, live (also known as "shell stock"), or already shucked (usually packed in half-pint or pint-size containers; note that the jarred "smalls" are actually more like medium-size oysters in the shell). Store oysters in the shell in a bowl, and drape a damp—not soaking wet—towel over them to keep them from drying out in the refrigerator. If I'm going to eat oysters raw, I buy them the day I want to eat them. That's just me, but it probably should be you too. If you buy them shucked, be sure to check the packing date and keep them in the coldest part of your refrigerator. I typically cook preshucked oysters.

....

hangtown fry

Hangtown fry was invented during the 1850s Gold Rush in Placerville, California, then known as Hangtown. Legend has it that a rich gold prospector coined the name when he demanded the most expensive dish at a local hotel. In those days, the costliest ingredients were bacon (from the East Coast), eggs (likely cormorant eggs delicately brought in from off the coast of San Francisco) and oysters (brought on ice or in saltwater barrels from the city). I've nicknamed this historically famous dish "Hangover Fry" because, well, it does the job—let's just leave it at that.

SERVES 4

8 strips thick-cut bacon

½ pint preshucked fresh oysters, preferably "small," or 1 dozen medium-size oysters in the shell, shucked‡

1 cup buttermilk

1 tablespoon unsalted butter

8 eggs

1½ cups roughly chopped arugula

½ teaspoon Tabasco

¼ cup half-and-half

Salt and freshly ground pepper

½ cup panko or bread crumbs

1 tablespoon high-heat vegetable oil

4 slices good crusty bread, toasted

4 lemon wedges, for garnish

Lay the bacon on an aluminum-foil-lined baking sheet. Place in the cold oven, then turn the oven on to 400°F and set the timer for 20 minutes. Soak the oysters in the buttermilk for 30 minutes in the refrigerator.

In the meantime, melt the butter in a large sauté pan over medium-low heat. Whisk the eggs with the arugula, Tabasco, and half-and-half. Season with salt and pepper and then pour the mixture into the pan. Grab a wooden spoon and start stirring. You will be tempted to turn the heat up, but don't. If you keep stirring the eggs at a medium-low temperature they will produce the creamiest, most delicious eggs you've ever had. It should take 8 to 10 minutes to set into small curds, but they will still have lots of moisture. Look for creamy, barely set eggs. When the eggs are done, place them at the back of the stove to keep warm.

When the bacon has finished cooking, remove it from the oven and set aside to drain on a paper-towel-lined plate. Drain the oysters and discard the buttermilk. Place the panko on a plate and dredge the oysters, coating them well on both sides.

(continued)

jet's oyster succotash

After a day spent scouring the beaches of southern Puget Sound for clams and oysters, my friends gathered together in my kitchen and a cooking frenzy ensued. My buddy Jet grabbed some corn and some herbs, and before long a version of this recipe was on the table: buttery, sweet, herbal, and smoky-salty. Oyster succotash goes from side dish to meal when you serve it with greens and some bruschetta. In the winter (since frozen edamame and corn are always available), it would be great alongside roasted chicken. In the summer, serve it with grilled flank steak or barbecued ribs.

SERVES 4 AS A SIDE DISH

In a large skillet over medium-high heat, cook the bacon until its fat is rendered and it is crisp, 6 to 7 minutes. Transfer the bacon with a slotted spoon to a paper-towel-lined plate, keeping the fat in the pan. Add the butter, shallots, and carrot. Sauté for 5 minutes, or until the vegetables are soft. Add the lemon thyme, edamame, and corn, and sauté until the corn caramelizes, another 2 to 3 minutes.

Deglaze the pan with the oyster liquid and reduce until the mixture is dry. Add the oysters, lemon juice, and white wine vinegar. Season to taste with salt, pepper, and Tabasco. Sprinkle with the parsley and the bacon.

* Edamame, or young soybeans in the pod, are sold in the frozen foods section of most supermarkets. You can also find shelled edamame, which are easy to thaw and add to recipes. If you have access to fresh fiddlehead ferns, you can use them in place of, or in combination with, the edamame. Salicornia, commonly known as beach asparagus or sea beans, would also be a lovely addition to this recipe, as would fava beans. All will need to be blanched in salted water for a few minutes then shocked in ice water before adding.

‡ Go to www.goodfishbook.com for a demonstration of how to shuck oysters.

PAIRING: A Chablis, such as Bouchard Aîné & Fils 2007, Burgundy, France, or a muscadet.

3 strips bacon, cut into small dice (about ⅓ cup)

2 tablespoons unsalted butter

¼ cup minced shallots

1 small carrot, cut into small dice (about ½ cup)

1 teaspoon minced fresh lemon thyme, or 1 teaspoon regular thyme plus ¼ teaspoon lemon zest

1 cup shelled edamame*

1 cup corn, thawed if using frozen

½ pint preshucked fresh oysters or 6 large oysters in the shell, shucked,‡ coarsely chopped and ¼ cup liquid reserved

1 teaspoon lemon juice

2 teaspoons white wine vinegar

Salt and freshly ground pepper

Tabasco

2 tablespoons minced fresh Italian parsley

– dungeness crab –

I love me some Dungeness crab—all ways, but especially pure and simple, where the shortest distance between two points is a straight line from a cracked crab to my mouth. Butter is always a nice accompaniment, but good Dungeness crab seems to contain its own oceany butter: rich yet still crisp and clean. (An extra bonus is its onboard sea salt seasoning.)

When I worked at The Herbfarm Restaurant, I used to pick up our live crabs from the fish market. That long drive out to Woodinville was always punctuated by quick peeks into my rearview mirror to see if an army of rogue crustaceans was plotting to hijack the car. They never did, which was a very good thing, because what a loss if I had missed out on transforming these crabby warriors into the dishes of chef Jerry Traunfeld's imaginings: paper-thin pasta squares enfolding crabmeat with a delicate lemon beurre blanc, herbed crab cocktails with shiso, and poofy, delicate crab soufflés.

CRAB THREE WAYS

When you need to buy Dungeness crabmeat you can go one of three ways:

1. *Purchase pre-cooked, cleaned, and picked crabmeat.* This is the most convenient option, but not necessarily the freshest option. Note that picked crabmeat has been picked from the crab but it might not have been picked through again for shell pieces, so do check it before using.

2. *Purchase pre-cooked whole crab.* You can ask the fishmonger to clean the crab for you, which means they will gut and rinse it. You will still have to crack and pick the meat yourself. This is an economical way to go.

3. *Purchase live crab.* Go to www.goodfishbook.com for a demonstration of how to cook and clean a crab. This option is desirable for the ultimate in freshness and gives you total control over the cooking process. This option is usually the same or slightly more expensive than buying pre-cooked whole crab.

A HELPFUL CONVERSION: Approximately one quarter of the crab's weight is meat, so if you need one pound of crabmeat, you'll need four pounds of whole crab.

dungeness crab panzanella with charred-tomato vinaigrette

I think if I had been given the following as a word problem in junior high, I might have actually rocked math: If a fabulous bread salad was on a train traveling east at 40 miles per hour, and a shipment of live Dungeness crabs was coming west traveling at 90 miles per hour, and just prior to impact someone threw some flaming tomatoes and fresh basil onto the tracks, how awesome would lunch be? You will have leftover dressing, which is a good thing, as you can spread it on toast, toss it with pasta or salad, serve it with Newspaper Crab with Three Sauces (page 53), or just eat it off a spoon.

SERVES 4 AS A LIGHT LUNCH

....

2 cups halved cherry or grape tomatoes

¼ cup plus 1 tablespoon extra-virgin olive oil

2 teaspoons balsamic vinegar

Salt and freshly ground pepper

½ cup roughly chopped fresh basil leaves

2½ cups crusty bread from a good artisan loaf, cut into medium cubes, crusts on

10 ounces Dungeness crabmeat

Preheat the broiler. Place a rack in the top third of the oven.

Toss the tomatoes with 1 tablespoon of the olive oil, 1 teaspoon of the balsamic vinegar, a pinch of salt, and a grind of pepper. Spread the tomatoes on a foil-lined baking sheet. Broil for 5 minutes, or until the tomatoes are charred in spots. Transfer to a bowl and set aside, leaving the broiler on.

Add half of the tomatoes to a blender, along with half of the basil, the remaining ¼ cup olive oil and 1 teaspoon balsamic vinegar, and another pinch of salt and grind of pepper. Blend until the dressing is smooth. Taste and adjust the seasoning if necessary.

Toss the bread cubes with 2 tablespoons of the dressing. Spread them on the baking sheet and broil until lightly crispy in places, about 5 minutes. Stir the cubes and broil for another minute or two, until they are crispy all over. Set aside.

Double-check the crabmeat for any stray bits of shell. Gently squeeze out any excess moisture with your hands. Toss the crab with 2 tablespoons of the dressing. To serve, mix the crab with the reserved bread cubes, reserved tomatoes, and 2 more tablespoons of the dressing. Add more salt and pepper if necessary, and garnish with the remaining basil leaves.

PAIRING: A sparkling rosé, such as Graham Beck Brut 2007, South Africa, or a still rosé.

newspaper crab with three sauces

One of my favorite things to do when friends come to Seattle for the first time is to take them to Pike Place Market, where we pick out cooked and cleaned crabs, grab some local microbrews from Pike Place Brewery, then jump in the car and head to the Queen Anne neighborhood. I've got the Sunday paper, a blanket, and lots of paper towels in the car, and we lay out a picnic at this little park that overlooks the entire Seattle skyline. If it is raining—which, this being Seattle, it is wont to do—I take my guests back to my house, where I completely gild the lily by accompanying the crab with several sauces. I'm sure you'll prefer one sauce over the others, but I've yet to meet anyone who didn't shamelessly lick the bottom of the soy caramel bowl.

SERVES 4 OUT-OF-TOWN GUESTS

4 cooked, cleaned Dungeness crabs

½ cup Soy Caramel Sauce (recipe follows)

½ cup Avocado Herb Sauce (recipe follows)

½ cup Lemon Panko Sauce (recipe follows)

Lay several sheets of newspaper out on the table along with plenty of napkins and various tools for cracking (crab crackers, rolling pins). Serve the crabs with larger shared or smaller individual bowls of each sauce for dipping.

PAIRING: A sauvignon blanc, such as Cliff Lede 2008, Napa Valley, California, or a light beer, such as Pike Place Brewery's Naughty Nellie.

SOY CARAMEL SAUCE

MAKES ABOUT ½ CUP

In a small saucepan, add the soy sauce, sake, mirin, sugar, and lemon juice. Bring to a boil over high heat, then lower the heat and reduce to a simmer. Cook the sauce until it is reduced by half, 5 to 7 minutes. Turn the heat down to its lowest setting and whisk in the butter 1 tablespoon at a time, adding each only after the previous one has melted. Taste and add more lemon juice if desired.

2 tablespoons soy sauce

¼ cup sake

3 tablespoons mirin

1 teaspoon sugar

1 tablespoon lemon juice

¼ cup (½ stick) cold unsalted butter, cut into tablespoons

Serve the chilled soup in shallow bowls with a small amount of crab salad in the middle. Lean a few of the larger crabmeat pieces against the salad. Drizzle some of the reserved coconut cream around the edges (thin the coconut cream with a little water if necessary).

PAIRING: A Washington riesling, such as Chateau Ste. Michelle Eroica 2008, Columbia Valley, or a German Kabinett riesling.

dungeness crab mac-and-cheese

If you get the chance to go crabbing and have yourself a good day, you're going to be in the enviable position of having a ton of crabmeat on your hands. That is the perfect time to pull out this recipe. Everyone loves mac-and-cheese, but adding sweet crabmeat—that's just ridiculously awesome. My secret for making this dish extra flavorful is to cook the pasta in the same water as I cooked the crab. As the pasta cooks, it absorbs the crab "stock," which then flavors the pasta from within.

SERVES 4 TO 6

....

Preheat the oven to 350°F. Grease a 13-by-9-inch baking dish with butter. Fill the sink with ice water.

Bring a large pot of salted water to a boil. Add the crabs. Once the water has returned to a boil, cook the crabs for 14 to 18 minutes. (Cook crabs that weigh around 2 pounds each, as most do, for about 14 minutes. Increase the cooking time by a few minutes if your crabs are larger.) While they cook, grate the cheddar and set aside. Using a pair of sturdy tongs, pull the crabs out of the cooking water and chill them in the ice water. Strain the crab cooking water through a colander, return it to the pot, and return to a boil.

In a large saucepan over medium-low heat, melt the butter and add the shallots. Cook for 1 minute. Whisk in the flour gradually and reduce the heat to low. Keep cooking and stirring the roux until it starts to smell nutty, about 5 minutes. Gradually add the milk while continuing to stir. Increase the heat to medium high and add the bay leaves, paprika, saffron, tomato paste, cayenne, and mustard. Simmer gently until the sauce is slightly thickened, about 10 minutes. Add the reserved cheese and cook until it has melted into the sauce. Taste for seasoning, then cover and set aside while you clean and crack the crabs.[‡]

Cook the pasta in the strained crab cooking water until it is al dente, drain, and transfer to a bowl. Stir the pasta and

2 to 3 live Dungeness crabs, or about ¾ pound crabmeat

1 pound good-quality cheddar cheese (I like a mix of medium and sharp)

¼ cup (½ stick) unsalted butter

¼ cup minced shallots

¼ cup all-purpose flour

3 cups whole milk, cold

2 fresh bay leaves, or 1 dried

¼ teaspoon regular or smoked paprika

⅛ teaspoon saffron, mixed with 1 tablespoon hot water

1 tablespoon tomato paste

⅛ teaspoon cayenne

2 teaspoons Dijon mustard

1 pound elbow or penne pasta

1 cup panko

1 tablespoon freshly grated lemon zest (about 1 large lemon)

¼ cup finely chopped fresh Italian parsley

¼ cup (½ stick) unsalted butter, melted

crabmeat into the sauce. Put this heart-stoppingly delicious concoction into the baking dish.

In a medium bowl, mix the panko with the lemon zest, parsley, and melted butter. Top the pasta with the panko mixture and bake for about 30 minutes, or until the mac-and-cheese is bubbly and browned on the top.

‡   Go to www.goodfishbook.com for a demonstration of how to clean live Dungeness crab.

PAIRING: A California chardonnay, such as Lioco 2007, Sonoma County, or a white Burgundy.

dungeness crab with bacon-cider sauce

This is a sophisticated dish that I pull out in the fall as a first course to impress my family from back East, especially when they start in on the "blue crab is better than Dungeness" rhetoric. If you live in the Pacific Northwest, it is highly likely that you can make this dish with ingredients raised or grown very close to home: world-famous Washington apples and cider, Pacific Dungies, and locally cured bacon.

SERVES 6 AS AN APPETIZER

1 pound Dungeness crabmeat

4 strips good-quality bacon, cut into small dice

1 apple, such as Gala or Granny Smith, sliced horizontally into four ⅓-inch slices through the core (remove the seeds with the tip of a knife, leaving the pretty star pattern)

⅓ cup small-diced onion

Pinch of salt

½ cup dry white wine

⅓ cup clam juice

¼ cup apple juice or cider

Heaping ¼ teaspoon freshly ground pepper

1 teaspoon minced fresh lemon thyme or regular thyme

1 tablespoon unsalted butter

1 teaspoon minced fresh tarragon

Cayenne (optional)

Maldon sea salt, for garnish (optional)

Double-check the crabmeat for any stray bits of shell. Place it in a medium bowl over another bowl partially filled with very hot tap water. Locate 4 nice, large leg pieces to use as a garnish and set aside. Cover the top bowl. After 5 minutes, give the crabmeat a gentle stir. You want it to be room temperature or slightly warm when you serve the dish.

In a small skillet over medium-high heat, add the bacon. Cook the bacon until its fat is rendered and it is crisp, about 10 minutes. Remove the bacon with a slotted spoon to a paper-towel-lined plate and set aside, reserving the fat. Pour the bacon fat through a fine mesh strainer into a cup. Clean the skillet and place it back on the stove over medium-high heat. Add the bacon fat back to the skillet and, when it is hot, carefully slip the apples into the pan. Fry them until one side is nicely caramelized, 3 to 4 minutes; then flip and cook them for 30 seconds more. Transfer them to a plate and keep warm.

Without cleaning the skillet, add the onions and salt, and cook over medium-high heat, scraping up any stuck-on bits. Cook until the onions are lightly browned, about 5 minutes. Deglaze the pan with the white wine, clam juice, and apple juice. Add the pepper and lemon thyme. Bring the sauce to a boil and reduce by half, about 5 minutes. Remove the skillet from the heat, then swirl in the butter, tarragon, and cayenne. Taste and check for seasoning.

(continued)

Serve each person a quarter of the crabmeat, placing it in the center of a warm plate. Place an apple slice (caramelized side up) to one side, leaning on the pile of crabmeat. Drizzle the sauce over the crab and apple, and garnish with some reserved bacon pieces and one piece of the reserved leg meat. Finish with a sprinkle of Maldon sea salt.

PAIRING: A Savennières, such as Château Pierre-Bise 2007, Loire Valley, France, or an Alsatian pinot gris.

– shrimp –

When I was just a wee lass, I had a thing bad for shrimp cocktail. This habit started when I was 6 or so—an age that required me to kneel on my seat at my family's favorite local restaurant to reach the shrimp that perched on the sides of a soda fountain glass. I remember how cold and frosty that glass was; how the ice cupped a thimbleful of cocktail sauce in the middle; how five plump shrimp fanned out from the center like the orange-pink petals of a rare flower.

I feel wistful about those cheap and easy shrimp cocktails, those family meals that seemed to be devoid of the modern conversations about food that are fairly commonplace today. Being an ethical eater sometimes gives me an adult-size headache and a penchant for sounding like an old fogie who starts sentences with, "Remember when . . . ?" I no longer eat shrimp in the numbers I used to. I've learned to anticipate—with joy—the seasons for food.

Thirty-some-odd years later, with the feeling of the wooden chair on my knees and the smell of lemon still etched in my nasal passages, I find myself at the docks in Anacortes, Washington, where I happen upon some live spot prawns being sold off a local boat. The sun is shining and the striped and spotted orange prawns are lookers, stunning against the blue sky. I hang my legs over the side of the dock and twist off the shrimp heads, thanking each one for its life. My excitement builds as I plan a menu—I'm thinking some cocktail sauce, a lemon, a tall frosty glass, some crushed ice. Yes, that feels about right.

— scallops —

If cooking seafood perfectly is the measure of a cook's skill, the scallop is a good measuring stick. Of all the things I've taught as a cooking instructor, it is the craft of perfectly searing a scallop that has most enthralled my students. No other seafood quite achieves its delicious duplicity: crispy, caramelized, sweet exterior meets creamy, silky, oceany interior.

In the male-dominated world of restaurant kitchens that I inhabited before venturing out on my own, I often found myself being measured up as I lowered scallops down into a smoking hot pan. Did I wince or cry out as hot drops of fat met the delicate skin of my forearm? Did I place the scallops too close together so that wisps of steam rose from the pan and attracted the glare of my sous chef? Did my lips curl into a very subtle smirk when I flipped the scallops over with a flick of the wrist to reveal, thankfully, a tawny brown glistening crust? You bet.

WHAT MAKES THIS A GOOD CHOICE: Sea scallops are filter feeders just like clams, mussels, and oysters; this process contributes to better water quality. Look for farmed Qualicum scallops from British Columbia. Like all farmed shellfish, scallops depend on clean waters to thrive, and as a result, shellfish farmers are often at the forefront of clean water advocacy initiatives. Weathervane scallops from Alaska are a second choice because they are harvested by mechanical dredge, which carries with it some habitat concerns that need to be more fully researched.

BY ANY OTHER NAME: Qualicum scallops (or "Qualicums") are a hybrid developed by Island Scallops Ltd. from the weathervane scallop (*Patinopecten caurinus*) and the Japanese scallop (*Patinopecten yessoensis*).

SEASON: Farmed scallops are available year-round (though they spawn from April to May). Weathervane scallop season in Alaska is from July through September, although very high-quality frozen weathervanes are available year-round.

BUYING TIPS: Some lesser scallops are soaked in sodium tripolyphosphate (STP), which can be used—or rather, abused—to minimize water loss when thawing frozen scallops. When applied to fresh scallops in excess, the scallops will take up extra moisture; more water equals diluted flavor and fewer scallops per pound. Buy "dry-packed" or "chemical-free," which is industry-speak for an unadulterated scallop. Dry-packed scallops will range from white to off-white to cream-colored: all are acceptable. Ask to smell the scallops: they should have a light, sweet ocean smell or hardly any at all. You'll find scallops sold in "count per pound" size designations. For example, large scallops are 10 to 20 per pound; medium scallops number 20 to 30 per pound. Of course, you'll pay more per pound for the larger scallops. For most of the recipes in this book, the size of the scallop doesn't matter. I only specify "large" in one recipe because using a single scallop for each serving is visually appealing.

QUESTIONS TO ASK BEFORE YOU PULL OUT YOUR WALLET: After asking where and when the scallops were harvested, the most important question is whether they are fresh or were previously frozen. I ask this question only because if I end up not using all the scallops that day, I will freeze some raw ones to use at a later date, but only if they haven't already been frozen (too many freezing and thawing cycles will destroy the texture).

....

CARING FOR YOUR GOOD FISH: Unwrap your scallops when you get them home. Place them on a paper-towel-lined plate and cover well with plastic wrap. Use them that day or the next. Remove the part of the adductor muscle that is sometimes still attached to the scallop, as it gets very tough when cooked. In the video about scallops at www.goodfishbook.com, I show you what this piece looks like and how to remove it.

....

HOW THIS TYPE OF SEAFOOD IS RAISED OR HARVESTED: Wild scallops can actually swim, pumping their adductor muscle to escape prey or move to a different area. They prefer to hang out in sand, gravel, and rock bottoms. Commercially farmed scallops are raised in net cages that are hung in the water column offshore. The scallops go from hatchery to harvest in 18 to 24 months.

....

SUSTAINABLE SUBSTITUTES: Crab and shrimp are good substitutes for scallops.

scallop crudo

Crudo is an Italian dish of raw fish dressed with olive oil, citrus, and sea salt. The beauty of a good crudo lies in its ability to preserve the subtlety of the fish flavor and bring out its richness with good olive oil while simultaneously balancing it with acid—in this case, orange juice. The best crudos have a textural component: here I use chopped bits of pumpkin seed and crunchy crystals of Maldon sea salt (worth seeking out at a specialty market or online if you've never had it).

SERVES 4 AS AN APPETIZER

½ pound sea scallops (see A Note on Eating Raw Seafood on page 235)

1 large orange

1 tablespoon lemon juice

Pinch of red pepper flakes

1 tablespoon chopped pumpkin seeds or pistachios, for garnish

4 teaspoons extra-virgin olive oil

1 teaspoon chopped fresh mint, for garnish

Maldon or gray sea salt

Place the scallops in a resealable plastic bag and freeze for 20 minutes to allow for easier slicing.

Zest the orange (you will have about 2½ tablespoons of zest). Cut a ⅛-inch horizontal slice from the middle of the orange. Trim off the remaining pith, then cut the orange flesh into small dice. Set aside. Squeeze the remaining orange to yield ⅓ cup juice.

In a small saucepan over high heat, bring the orange juice, orange zest, lemon juice, and red pepper flakes to a boil. Cook the mixture until it reduces to a syrup (about 2 tablespoons remaining), about 3 minutes. Pour through a fine mesh strainer, pressing on the zest to release its oil into the syrup. Discard the solids and allow the syrup to cool.

Toast the pumpkin seeds in a small skillet over high heat, stirring constantly, until they smell toasted and darken in color, about 2 minutes.

Using a very sharp, thin-bladed slicing knife, cut the scallops horizontally (against the grain) into ⅛-inch slices. Arrange the slices decoratively on 4 small plates. Spoon equal amounts of the syrup over the scallops. Drizzle approximately 1 teaspoon of the olive oil over each portion. Garnish with a sprinkling of pumpkin seeds, reserved diced orange, and mint. Carefully distribute a small pinch of Maldon salt over the scallop slices. Serve immediately.

PAIRING: A sauvignon blanc, such as DiStefano 2008, Columbia Valley, Washington, or an Australian riesling.

scallops, grits, and greens

For the greens:

1 tablespoon extra-virgin olive oil

1 bunch kale, stems removed, leaves chopped into bite-size pieces

1 bunch mustard greens, stems removed, leaves chopped into bite-size pieces

Pinch of red pepper flakes

¼ teaspoon salt

2 teaspoons honey

1 tablespoon apple cider vinegar

½ cup chicken or pork stock

For the grits:

2 cups whole milk

2 cups chicken or pork stock

¼ teaspoon salt

½ cup quick-cooking grits or polenta

1 cup (about 2 ounces) grated cheddar cheese

1 teaspoon orange zest

For the scallops:

1 pound sea scallops

1 tablespoon ancho chile powder* (or chile powder of your choice)

Salt and freshly ground pepper

1 tablespoon high-heat vegetable oil

You've probably heard of shrimp and grits, but what about scallops and grits? I wondered why I'd never thought of this dish or eaten it before. The sweet, caramelized scallop crust with a buttery soft interior mirrors the creaminess of the cheesy grits combined with earthy, spicy greens mellowed with honey. Turns out that this dish is a culinary oversight needing immediate rectification.

SERVES 4

....

To prepare the greens, in a large pot over medium-high heat, add all of its ingredients. Stir well, cover, and cook for 10 to 15 minutes, or until the greens are tender. Taste for seasoning and adjust as needed. Keep warm.

To prepare the grits, in a large saucepan over high heat, add the milk, chicken stock, and salt. Bring to a boil and then reduce the heat to maintain a simmer. Gradually whisk in the grits. Reduce the heat to medium low and stir the grits for 5 minutes, or until they are creamy and tender. Stir in the cheddar and orange zest. Keep warm.

To prepare the scallops, dry them with paper towels. Place them on a plate and season with the chile powder, salt, and pepper. Heat a heavy skillet over high heat. Add the vegetable oil and, when it is really hot, carefully add the scallops to the pan, being careful not to splatter oil on yourself or crowd the pan with too many scallops. Cook the scallops for 2 minutes on one side without disturbing them, or until they are caramelized, then flip, cooking the other side for only a minute or so more.

To serve, scoop the grits onto a platter or plates. Top with the greens and scallops.

*   Look for ancho chile powder in the Mexican section of large supermarkets. You can also grind dried ancho chiles in a spice grinder to make your own powder.

PAIRING: You *must* drink Red Stripe Jamaican lager with this dish.

scallops with carrot cream and marjoram

About ten years ago, at Tulio Ristorante in downtown Seattle, I had a memorable pasta dish featuring the herb marjoram; it was just a small, fragrant amount tossed with butter and fresh pasta, but so many years later I can still smell its perfume. Oregano's sexier sister, as marjoram is sometimes called, is also a favorite of Jerry Traunfeld, former executive chef at The Herbfarm Restaurant, who taught me to combine it with carrots. There is something about the earthy sweetness of carrots paired with the delicate pine notes of marjoram that really works. The addition of sweet, briny scallops to that already solid combination blows this dish right out of the water.

SERVES 4 AS AN APPETIZER

To prepare the carrot cream, add the carrots and salt to a medium saucepan and cover with water. Bring to a boil and cook for 7 to 8 minutes, or until the carrots are tender. Drain the carrots and add them to a blender along with the cream and a pinch of pepper to taste. Blend until the mixture is a very smooth purée and set aside.

To prepare the pickled carrots, in a medium bowl, toss the carrots with the rice wine vinegar. Marinate the carrots for at least 20 minutes. Drain, reserving the vinegar for another use, and set aside.

To prepare the scallops, dry them with paper towels. Place them on a plate and season generously with salt and pepper. Heat a heavy skillet over high heat. Add the vegetable oil and, when it is really hot, carefully add the scallops to the pan, being careful not to splatter oil on yourself or crowd the pan with too many scallops. Cook the scallops for 2 minutes on one side without disturbing them, or until they are caramelized, then flip, cooking the other side for only a minute or so more.

To assemble the dish, gently reheat the carrot cream, then spoon some on each of 4 plates. Top each plate with several scallops. Drizzle some Herb Oil around the scallops and garnish with a sprinkling of pickled carrots and marjoram leaves.

PAIRING: A sauvignon blanc, such as Château Leredde Sancerre Blanc 2007, Sancerre, France, or a Chablis.

For the carrot cream:

½ pound carrots, cut into large dice (about 2 cups)

1 teaspoon salt

½ cup cream

Freshly ground pepper

For the pickled carrots:

1 large carrot, sliced into short ribbons using a vegetable peeler (about 1 cup)

¼ cup seasoned rice wine vinegar

For the scallops:

1 pound sea scallops

Salt and freshly ground pepper

1 tablespoon high-heat vegetable oil

For serving:

2 tablespoons Herb Oil (recipe follows)

1 teaspoon marjoram leaves, for garnish

For the scallops:

4 large (10 to 20 count) sea scallops, about 1½ ounces per scallop

Salt and freshly ground pepper

1 tablespoon high-heat vegetable oil

For serving:

1 teaspoon fresh tarragon leaves, as garnish

To prepare the beurre blanc, in a small saucepan over high heat, add the tarragon, shallot, white wine, and champagne vinegar. Bring to a boil, then reduce the heat to a simmer and cook until the liquid is reduced to just 1 tablespoon, 6 to 7 minutes. Turn the heat down to its lowest setting and whisk in the cold butter 1 tablespoon at a time, adding each only after the previous one has been incorporated. Taste for seasoning and then set the beurre blanc aside in a warm place. It will hold for about half an hour; if it should "break," mix it in a blender for 1 minute to re-emulsify.

To prepare the vegetable sauté, in a sauté pan over medium heat, add the prosciutto. Cook the prosciutto until its fat is rendered and it starts to crisp, 6 to 8 minutes. Add the shallots and asparagus tips and cook for another 2 to 3 minutes, or until the shallots are tender. Add the reserved peas. Season to taste with salt and pepper. Set aside and keep warm.

To prepare the scallops, dry them with paper towels. Place them on a plate and season generously with salt and pepper. Heat a heavy skillet over high heat. Add the vegetable oil and, when it is really hot, carefully add the scallops to the pan, being careful not to splatter oil on yourself or crowd the pan with too many scallops. Cook the scallops for 3 minutes on one side without disturbing them, or until they are caramelized, then flip, cooking the other side for 2 minutes more. Set aside and keep warm until ready to assemble dish.

To assemble the dish, place a little pea and asparagus purée on each of 4 plates. Top with some of the prosciutto, pea, and asparagus sauté and a seared scallop. Pour some tarragon beurre blanc over the scallop. Garnish with tarragon leaves.

PAIRING: A grüner veltliner, such as F.X. Pichler Federspiel Loibner Frauenweingarten 2007, Wachau, Austria, or a white Bordeaux.

FINFISH

KING

KING / CHINO

SOCKEYE

COHO / SILVE

KETA / CHU

— wild salmon —

In 2006 I ran the galley of a seventy-five-foot yacht headed up to Ketchikan, Alaska, by way of the Inside Passage. My sole motivation for taking this job—aside, of course, from the stunningly beautiful landscapes—was what I had hoped would be access to some of the freshest and most delicious seafood I'd ever laid my hands on. I was not disappointed.

The boat was a day outside Queen Charlotte Sound and its nauseatingly rolling sea. When we arrived at the Shearwater Marina, near Bella Bella, British Columbia, my sea legs were barely beneath me, so the dock planks felt especially comforting. Matt, the marina manager, greeted me on the dock and quickly offered me a freshly caught twenty-pound king salmon that some sport fishermen had left them that day. By way of an answer, I jogged up the dock, trailing after him, a smile on my face like a delightfully simple-minded Labrador retriever. I remember holding that salmon tenderly to my chest, thanking him profusely, and coddling it the whole way back to the boat, grinning like an idiot.

I busily got to work cleaning, scaling, and cutting the salmon into portions that would fit in the boat's refrigerator and freezer. I threw the backbone and tail over the side of the boat and watched as little fish instantaneously darted at it, taking their share as it slowly descended. I watched the bones sink until I could no longer see them and then caught up with the rest of the group. I smelled like a salmon. I couldn't have been happier.

grilled sockeye salmon with fennel two ways

When I was a child, I despised black jellybeans. I went so far as to think of them as assault weapons designed by adults to keep the candy bowl away from the children (see also: Good & Plentys and black licorice drops). But tastes change, children mature into adults, and suddenly I'm the one foisting licorice-tasting fennel onto children's plates. Fennel has become my favorite vegetable, next to kale; it marries perfectly with the strong character and richness of wild salmon. In this recipe, it is featured two ways: as a fennel salt rub and in wedges, smoky and sweet from the grill.

SERVES 4

To prepare the fennel salt, grind the fennel seeds, salt, and peppercorns together in a spice grinder. Reserve.

To prepare the vegetables, in a medium bowl, toss the fennel and onion with the olive oil and 1 teaspoon of the fennel salt.

To prepare the salad, in a small bowl combine the yogurt, mustard, cayenne, and honey. Season to taste with salt. Right before serving, lightly coat the greens with 2 tablespoons of the dressing. Reserve the rest to use as a sauce for the salmon.

To prepare the salmon, remove the pin bones.[‡] Coat the salmon pieces on all sides with the remaining fennel salt and set them aside on a plate in the refrigerator.

Preheat an outdoor gas grill or indoor grill pan to high heat. Oil the grill rack with vegetable oil.

Grill the fennel wedges and onion slices for 6 to 8 minutes, or until crisp-tender. Grill the salmon, skin side up, until the grill marks are clearly visible. Sockeye is usually fairly thin, so a ½-inch thick piece should cook for 2 to 3 minutes per side.

(continued)

For the fennel salt:

1 tablespoon dried fennel seeds

1 teaspoon salt

½ teaspoon black peppercorns

For the vegetables:

1 large fennel bulb, stems removed, cut into thin wedges, small frond pieces reserved for garnish

1 red onion, cut into thick slices

1 tablespoon extra-virgin olive oil

For the salad:

¼ cup plain Greek-style yogurt

1 teaspoon Dijon mustard

Pinch of cayenne

½ teaspoon honey

Salt

4 cups salad greens (mixture of arugula, frisée, mizuna etc.)

For the salmon:

1 pound sockeye salmon fillet, skin on, cut into 4 equal portions

Vegetable oil, for oiling the grill

In an ovenproof skillet over high heat, add the vegetable oil. When it is hot, carefully add the salmon fillets, skin side up. Cook for 2 to 3 minutes, or until the fillets are browned, then flip them carefully and place the skillet in the oven for 5 to 6 more minutes (assuming the fish is about an inch high measured at the thickest point). Ideally, the salmon should be served medium rare.

To serve, divide the greens and beans among 4 bowls and top each with a piece of salmon. Ladle some of the coconut "pot liquor" all around the outer edge of the bowl. Tuck some sweet potatoes alongside the salmon and garnish with a lime wedge.

PAIRING: A viognier, such as Kunin "Stolpman Vineyard" 2006, Central Coast, California, or an Alsatian pinot gris.

roasted salmon with morels and pinot noir sauce

For the pinot noir sauce:

¼ cup minced shallots

1 teaspoon fennel seeds, lightly crushed with the side of a knife

1 star anise pod

2 teaspoons honey

1 bottle pinot noir

4 cups vegetable or chicken stock

For the vegetables:

1 large turnip or rutabaga, cut into medium dice

1 tablespoon extra-virgin olive oil, plus additional for drizzling

1 teaspoon salt

Freshly ground pepper

1 small leek, cut into medium dice

3 ounces morel mushrooms, cleaned well and halved lengthwise (about 1 cup)

For the roasted salmon:

1 pound wild king salmon fillet, skinned, pin bones removed,‡ and cut into 4 equal portions

2 tablespoons extra-virgin olive oil

Salt

For finishing:

1 cup (2 sticks) cold unsalted butter, cut into large dice

I once thought butter sauces were a cop-out. Of course it tastes great, it's a butter sauce! On principle, I wouldn't make one. Then I got older and realized that the French didn't build their civilization upon the semifirm back of butter and barrels of wine on a whim. Sure, first there was that cook who drunkenly tipped his Burgundy into the butter pot, but then they codified that drunken miracle into the very fabric of their cuisine. We are all the beneficiaries of this legacy, and it was naïve bluster that kept me from embracing dishes such as this one, where copious amounts of pinot noir meet butter, coating and enhancing the fatty goodness of a perfectly cooked piece of salmon. The earthy morel mushrooms and sweet leeks heighten this recipe and throw it completely over the top.

SERVES 4

To prepare the sauce, in a wide saucepan over high heat, combine all of the sauce ingredients. Bring the liquid to a boil, then reduce the heat to a gentle simmer. Reduce the sauce until you have 1½ cups, about 40 minutes. While the sauce reduces, prepare the vegetables.

Preheat the oven to 400°F.

To prepare the vegetables, spread the turnips on a baking sheet lined with parchment paper. Drizzle with 1 tablespoon olive oil, add the salt, and season to taste with pepper. Cover the turnips with foil and roast in the oven for 20 minutes. Uncover the turnips, add the leeks and morels, and stir well. Drizzle with a little more olive oil, season to taste with salt and pepper, and roast the vegetables, uncovered, for 20 more minutes. Remove the baking sheet from the oven, cover with foil, and set aside. Turn the oven temperature down to 250°F.

To prepare the salmon, lay the salmon pieces on a baking sheet lined with parchment paper. Rub them with the olive oil and season with salt. When the oven has cooled to 250°F, roast the salmon for 10 to 12 minutes, or until a gentle push on the top just reveals flaking (see page 102). It is best served on the rare side. Keep it warm, tented with foil, while you finish the sauce.

To finish the sauce, first strain it through a fine-mesh sieve. Return the sauce to the saucepan over medium-low heat. Whisk the cold butter into the sauce a little at a time.

To serve, spoon a small amount of sauce onto each plate and top with the vegetables and salmon.

‡ Go to www.goodfishbook.com for a demonstration of how to remove the skin from a fillet and remove pin bones.

PAIRING: A Burgundy, such as Albert Bichot Vieilles Vignes Pinot Noir Bourgogne 2007, or a Chinon.

— pacific halibut —

My first dealings with a whole halibut came soon after a career change, having bailed early on a track toward medical school. I chose sautéing over surgery, though I was pleased when I realized that white jackets, knife work, and a certain amount of blood were still in my future. I was a third-quarter culinary student when my chef-instructor heaved a large halibut up onto a stainless steel worktable. I learned that day that a "fletch" is a halibut fillet (there are four, unlike round fish, such as a salmon, which have two). I sharpened my knives and joined my fellow students in filleting the big beast, two fletches on the top, flip, two fletches on the bottom.

That halibut went through an early career change of sorts as well. A halibut starts its life as a round fish with an eye on either side of its head, as you might expect. However, by the time a halibut is six months old, it has settled down to the bottom of the ocean and made a transition to life as a flatfish. From then on both eyes—having shifted to the top side of its body—stare up at the world swimming by. This life change seems to suit the halibut, and I can say the same for myself. I chose the right career, shifting my gaze toward a life in food, and I, too, have never looked back.

halibut tacos with tequila-lime marinade and red cabbage slaw

I present to you the godfather of fish tacos that I wait all winter for, pining longingly for the spring season when the first wild Alaska halibut comes to market. If you have a bit more time, make some homemade guacamole. It is painfully simple: smash 2 ripe avocados with a fork, and add 1½ tablespoons lime juice, ¾ teaspoon salt, and 1 teaspoon hot sauce of your choice—mine is Tabasco.

SERVES 4

....

To prepare the slaw, toss the cabbage with the salt. Place in a colander. Locate a bowl that will fit nicely into the colander, fill it with water, and set it on top of the cabbage. Set this in the sink. The weight of the bowl of water will help force water from the cabbage, concentrating its flavor.

Lightly press the grated apple to drain any excess liquid. In a large bowl, mix the apple with the mustard seeds, cilantro, apple cider vinegar, and olive oil. Give the cabbage a squeeze with those fancy kitchen tools of yours called "hands." Rinse the salt off the cabbage and squeeze again, getting all the liquid out. Combine the cabbage with the rest of the slaw ingredients and season to taste with salt. Set aside.

To prepare the marinade, combine all of its ingredients in a small bowl.

To prepare the halibut, place it in a large pan. Pour the marinade over the fillet and set aside for 20 minutes.

In a grill pan or sauté pan over high heat, add the vegetable oil. Add the halibut, reserving the marinade, and cook until the fish is browned on one side, about 3 to 4 minutes. Flip the halibut carefully and continue cooking until the fish is thinking about flaking, but not quite yet flaking (see page 102), about 8 minutes per inch of fish (measured at its thickest point). The fish will continue to cook a bit more after you take it from the heat. Transfer the fish to a platter. Add the marinade to

For the red cabbage slaw:

¾ pound red cabbage, shredded (about 4 cups)

1 tablespoon kosher salt

1 Granny Smith apple, cored and grated

½ teaspoon mustard seeds

½ bunch cilantro leaves and stems, roughly chopped (about ¾ cup)

2 tablespoons apple cider vinegar

2 tablespoons extra-virgin olive oil

For the tequila-lime marinade:

1 lime, first zested, then juiced (about 1 teaspoon zest and 2 tablespoons juice)

2 tablespoons tequila*

½ teaspoon salt

2 small jalapeños, halved, seeds and membranes removed, sliced crosswise into half rings

1 small red onion, cut into thin half moons (about ⅔ cup)

2 tablespoons extra-virgin olive oil

For the halibut:

1 pound halibut fillet, skinned‡

1 tablespoon high-heat vegetable oil

For the topping:

1 teaspoon vegetable oil

4 Fresno chiles, seeded and minced

2 tablespoons minced red onion

⅓ cup chopped cilantro leaves

2 limes, peeled and flesh cut into small dice

Salt

To prepare the topping, heat the vegetable oil in a small sauté pan over medium-high heat. Fry the chiles and onion until they are caramelized, about 10 minutes. Remove from the heat and stir in the cilantro and lime. Season to taste with salt. Serve a spoonful on top of each person's curry.

* Kaffir lime leaves are sold fresh in Asian markets. They freeze well, so buy extra leaves for future use.

‡ Go to www.goodfishbook.com for a demonstration of how to remove the skin from a fillet.

PAIRING: A German riesling, such as Joh. Jos. Christoffel Erben, Ürziger Würzgarten, Spätlese 2006, Mosel, or an Alsatian gewürztraminer.

1¼ cups packed nettle leaves*

2 pounds (about 2 large) russet potatoes

1 egg, beaten

¾ cup all-purpose flour, plus additional for kneading

¼ teaspoon salt

NETTLE GNOCCHI

SERVES 4 TO 6

Preheat the oven to 350°F.

To prepare the nettles for both the gnocchi and the sauce, bring a large pot of water to a boil. While the water heats, fill a medium bowl with ice water. When the water is boiling, using gloves or tongs, carefully add the nettles, making sure they are submerged. Cook for exactly 5 minutes. Remove them immediately with a slotted spoon or tongs and plunge them into the ice bath. When the nettles have cooled, remove them from the ice bath and with your hands squeeze out all the water. Finely chop the nettles. Divide into two portions: set aside ¼ cup for making the gnocchi and reserve 1 cup for making the sauce.

Pierce the potatoes all over with the tines of a fork. Bake them in the oven directly on a rack for about 1 hour, flipping them after 30 minutes, until they are tender. While they are still hot (and using towels to protect yourself), slip the potato skins from the potato and discard. Run the potato and nettles through a ricer or food mill, or mash the potatoes really well by hand and then mash the nettles into the potatoes. Cool on a baking sheet.

When the potatoes are cool, transfer them to a bowl and stir in the egg, flour, and salt. Mix well with a wooden spoon and then knead the dough in the bowl until it forms a ball, adding more flour if necessary. Transfer the dough to a wooden board and divide it into 8 pieces. Roll each piece into a long rope about ¾ inch in diameter. When all the pieces are rolled out, cut each rope into gnocchi approximately ¾-inch long. If desired, use a fork to press down the gnocchi, lightly dragging it back to shape them. For a different look, you can pick up the gnocchi and roll them off the tines of the fork.

To freeze the gnocchi for later use, place them on a parchment-paper-lined baking sheet (make sure they are not touching each other), and put them in the freezer for about 1 hour. When the gnocchi are frozen, transfer them to a resealable plastic bag and use within 3 months.

If cooking the gnocchi immediately, bring a large pot of water to a boil. Season the water generously with salt and add the gnocchi in batches. Cook until they float to the surface and then, after about 1 minute, taste one: it should be light and fluffy, not dense. Cook a little longer if necessary; then, using a slotted spoon, transfer the gnocchi to a bowl.

If you are not serving them right away, drizzle the gnocchi with some olive oil or butter to keep them from sticking together. Or transfer the cooked gnocchi immediately into a sauté pan to brown them.

* See the note about nettles on page 129.

HOW TO SMOKE FISH AT HOME

If you have an actual, legitimate smoker, I'm jealous! For the rest of us: you can turn a wok into a makeshift smoker. I recommend doing this in an outdoor grill if you don't have a good kitchen fan. (But if you do, turn on the fan, disable your smoke alarm, open a few windows, and get started.)

Set the wok over high heat. Place about ½ cup soaked wood chips (I prefer apple wood or alder) in the bottom of the wok. I use a propane torch to quickly ignite the chips, then I leave them to burn for about 1 minute, blow out the flames, cover the wok, and allow it to fill with smoke (about 2 minutes). Lacking a torch, you can instead simply cover the wok and wait for the high heat to get the wood smoking (this will take a little longer, 3 to 4 minutes). Once the wok is filled with smoke, carefully lay a circular rack (sprayed or brushed with oil) inside the wok. Season your fish with salt and pepper. Lay the fish carefully on the rack. Cover and smoke the fish over high heat for 8 to 9 minutes per inch of fish (measured at its thickest point). You'll see the flesh turn a nice golden color when the smoke has penetrated. This method is called "hot-smoking," which cooks the fish all the way through.

— black cod —

Names are secondary to experiences when you're a child. Somewhere deep down in my childhood mind I might have known the fish I kept returning to was called sablefish, but that seemed beside the point. The point was reaching across the table with fork extended before my stupid brothers could take it all.

Sablefish was brought to our family table in what we called "the spread." The spread happened when Uncle Vic and Aunt Selly would come in from "the city" (New York) and bring with them "the fixin's" from Russ and Daughters. There would be bialys and bagels, sablefish and whitefish, herring, lox, and pickles. My grandmother would contribute onions, cream cheese, wedges of lemon, black olives, and big slices of her garden tomatoes. Bagel sandwiches would get piled so high we couldn't stuff them in our mouths and instead had to deconstruct them with knife and fork. The spread, the accompaniments, the extended family around my grandparent's big dining room table—this is what I think of when I taste black cod.

It wasn't until years later that I realized sablefish and black cod are the same thing. In fact, I do believe I've said at a cocktail party or two that my two favorite fish were sablefish and black cod. At least I'm consistent.

roasted black cod with bok choy and soy caramel sauce

Typically when I develop a recipe, I do my utmost to roll out a red carpet for the star ingredient. I may add other ingredients to boost the star, but it's clear they play second fiddle. A great piece of fish deserves top billing. Herbs, spices, and sauces are relegated to the role of supporting cast—until now. Let me be frank: this dish is all about the soy caramel. It was always all about the soy caramel. The black cod is merely a delicious platform on which the sauce sits. The bok choy and cabbage are vegetal intermissions. When the house lights dim, the soy caramel upstages them all.

SERVES 4

Preheat the oven to 400°F. Line a sheet pan with aluminum foil.

You're going to make 4 separate piles on the foil. Each pile will get ½ cup cabbage, a bok choy half, a tomato half sprinkled with a little salt, and a quarter of the green onions. Drizzle each pile with 1 teaspoon sesame oil and 1 teaspoon rice wine vinegar. Top with a lime slice and sprinkle with some chile pieces. Roast the vegetables in the oven for 20 minutes, or until they are soft and lightly browned around the edges. Keep the oven on.

Remove the pan from the oven, place one piece of black cod, skin side down, on each pile, and drizzle 1 tablespoon soy caramel sauce on each piece of fish. Roast for another 8 to 10 minutes or until a press of the finger reveals a sliding away, ever so gently, of the fish into the beginning of individual flakes. Serve with the rice and remaining soy caramel sauce.

PAIRING: An Oregon pinot gris, such as Eyrie Vineyards 2007, Willamette Valley, or a Savennières from the Loire Valley in France.

5 ounces red cabbage, thinly sliced (about 2 cups)

2 large bulbs bok choy, halved

2 small tomatoes, halved

Salt

4 green onions, white and green parts cut into 3-inch lengths

4 teaspoons toasted sesame oil

4 teaspoons seasoned rice wine vinegar

4 slices lime

1 serrano chile, sliced (optional)

1 pound black cod fillet or steaks, cut into 4 equal portions

½ cup Soy Caramel Sauce (page 53)

4 cups cooked rice

sake-steamed black cod with ginger and sesame

1 pound black cod fillet, cut into 4 equal portions

Salt and freshly ground pepper

1 cup sake

1 cup water

1 tablespoon soy sauce

1 tablespoon grated fresh ginger

2 teaspoons plus ¼ teaspoon toasted sesame oil

8 ounces (about 4 cups) fresh spinach

¼ cup thinly sliced radishes

1 tablespoon plus 2 teaspoons seasoned rice wine vinegar

1 tablespoon sesame seeds

½ teaspoon sugar

Black cod is an extremely rich fish, full of good omega-3 fatty acids, and therefore kind to novice cooks, as it is hard to overcook. I developed this recipe to downplay the black cod's natural fattiness for a night when you want a lighter meal. The fish and spinach are steamed and served with the sake-infused steaming liquid and a quick radish-and-sesame pickle.

SERVES 4

Season the black cod generously with salt and pepper.

Add the sake, water, soy sauce, ginger, and 2 teaspoons of the sesame oil to a pot with a steamer insert (you could use your pasta pot and insert). Bring to a boil and then reduce the heat to a simmer. Simmer for 5 minutes. Add the spinach to the steamer insert (making sure the liquid is below the bottom of the insert), cover the pot, and steam the spinach for 5 to 7 minutes, or until wilted. Remove the spinach and set aside to cool. Turn off the heat, leaving the sake broth in the bottom of the pot.

In a small bowl, mix the radishes with 1 tablespoon of the rice wine vinegar. Let the radishes marinate until you are ready to serve.

Squeeze all of the liquid out of the spinach with your hands, and chop it into bite-size pieces. In a small sauté pan, toast the sesame seeds over medium-high heat until lightly browned and fragrant, about 3 minutes. Reserve 1 teaspoon for garnish. Grind the rest of the sesame seeds with the sugar in a spice grinder or mortar and pestle. Transfer to a small bowl and stir in 1 tablespoon of the sake broth, the remaining 2 teaspoons rice wine vinegar, a pinch of salt, and the remaining ¼ teaspoon sesame oil. Toss the spinach with this dressing. Place the spinach in a deep, wide serving bowl and cover to keep warm. Set aside.

Bring the sake broth back to a boil. Place the black cod pieces on the steamer insert and place over the boiling liquid. Cover the pot and steam the fish for 9 minutes per inch of fish (measured at its thickest point). The fish is done when a press of the finger reveals a sliding away, ever so gently, of the fish into the beginning of individual flakes.

To serve, top the spinach with the steamed black cod. Pour some of the sake broth over the fish and around the spinach. Squeeze the rice wine vinegar from the radishes and mix them with the reserved teaspoon of sesame seeds. Garnish the fish with the radish-sesame pickle.

PAIRING: Junmai-shu sake or gewürztraminer.

For

¾ c

2 ta
  sh

1 te
  gi

1½

¼ te

¼ c
  ve

For

1 po
  int

1 ta

1½

For
sala

3 ta
  wi

1 ta

2 te
  gi

1 te
  ch

2 ta
  on

1½ t
  fre
  ch

1 En
  ler
  int

For

2 fre
  ve

— rainbow trout —

I went trout fishing for the first time last summer, though the use of the word "trout" might be a tad bit generous. Technically I caught more trees, shrubs, and other anglers' lines than I did trout. My wife, April, is the angler in our household. She grew up in Eastern Oregon, in a small town called La Grande. Her first trout-fishing trip was at 5 years old. As the only girl with two older brothers, she was being given a reprieve from icky "girl" activities, like playing house and dressing up dolls.

Her older brother played patient and bemused teacher as she cast her first line onto her shirt. He laughed and detached the hook, pointed her shoulders in the right direction, and ducked as she sent her first successful cast into the lake. She stood back and acted as watchful sentry over that bobber, looking for any whisper of movement. Before too long that bobber disappeared under the water and then popped back up with a little dance. She tried to pull the fish in, but it appeared to have the upper hand. Her brother got the better of it and declared that trout to be, by far, the biggest catch of the whole trip.

For years afterward, April would beg her father to take her fishing. Father and daughter would set up their stools, place a forked stick in the ground, and lean their poles in the crook. They'd commune in silence ("shhh—the fish will hear us!" he'd warn her), staring out at the lake, a world of action beneath the illusion of stillness. April let me fish with her father's pole this summer; we spent an entire day sharing the silence while I carefully baited the hook, cast the line just so, and then reeled in branch after branch after branch. April kindly didn't say a word.

cast-iron rainbow trout

I learned how to make this dish when I cooked at La Spiga in Seattle. I loved its simplicity and earthy flavors: nutty trout, woodsy mushrooms (chanterelles are amazing in this recipe), smoky bacon, piney sage, and bright wine. You can serve the trout on a platter, but sometimes I'll transfer the fillets and sauce back to the skillet and serve it that way—the residual heat retained in the iron keeps the dish warm.

SERVES 4

½ ounce (½ cup) dried wild mushrooms, or 3 ounces (1 cup) fresh wild mushrooms

Two (1-pound) whole rainbow trout, filleted‡; heads, tails, and ribs removed

Salt and freshly ground pepper

All-purpose flour, for dusting the fillets

3 strips bacon, cut into small dice (about ½ cup)

High-heat vegetable oil, for frying

¼ cup small, whole fresh sage leaves

½ cup dry white wine

Preheat the oven to 200°F.

If using dried wild mushrooms, rehydrate them in 1 cup of very hot tap water. Place a small bowl on top of the mushrooms to keep them submerged. Let them sit for 30 minutes while you prepare the rest of the ingredients. If using fresh mushrooms, remove any grit by gently brushing or washing them, then cut into bite-size pieces.

Season the trout fillets with salt and pepper. Dust them with the flour on both sides, shaking off any excess.

Heat a cast-iron skillet over medium heat. Add the bacon and cook until its fat is rendered and it is crisp, 7 to 8 minutes. Transfer the bacon with a slotted spoon to a paper-towel-lined plate and set aside, reserving the fat. Turn the heat up to high. When the pan is very hot, fry the trout fillets, skin side up, for about 2 minutes, then flip and cook for another 2 minutes, or just until the fillets brown. Transfer each fillet to an oven-proof platter and keep warm in the oven while you fry the remaining fish (add the vegetable oil, 1 tablespoon at a time, if the pan is dry).

(continued)

— albacore tuna —

I stared blankly at my friend, trying to look knowledgeable. She asked me if I wanted to go in on buying whole local albacore tuna and wondered if I would teach her how to fillet it, which, admittedly, I had never done before. The fish were coming in whole and ungutted off a local boat. "Sure," I told her, "I'd love to," and then I hurried off to spend an hour on YouTube, where I found numerous people with wildly different techniques for filleting whole tuna. I picked up a few tips and then sharpened my knives. I pantomimed my attack strategy, looking more like a demented ninja with an inadequate sword than a seasoned albacore filleter.

The day came and I met my friends at Fishermen's Terminal, where we selected whole fish directly off the boat. On a hot August afternoon we set up a makeshift albacore-processing line. We all took a turn practicing the techniques of gutting, cleaning, skinning, and filleting. It was messy work and "fragrant" at that (gutting fish carries with it a certain special value-added olfactory experience). I saved a few heads for crab bait, and we buried the bones and tails in the yard, deep enough so the dogs wouldn't find this special treat. The loins, four beautiful rosy pink cuts per fish, were vacuum-sealed in bags marked for our different freezers and packed on ice in coolers. We toasted our stinky, messy selves with a cold, crisp beer, while flies buzzed over our heads, mistaking us for dead fish. And really, who could blame them?

There are a couple of ways to serve this dish. You can lay the albacore slices on a platter, place the Dandelion Crackers in a basket, and pass the lime cream around for people to assemble as they wish. Alternatively, you can break the Dandelion Crackers into bite-size pieces, place an albacore slice on top, and garnish with a small dollop of lime cream.

PAIRING: A sauvignon blanc, such as Efeste "Feral" 2008, Columbia Valley, Washington, or a gin and tonic, naturally.

....

DANDELION CRACKERS

MAKES 6 EXTRA-LARGE CRACKERS

In a medium bowl, whisk together the flours, salt, and sugar. Add the water, olive oil, and dandelion petals. In a stand mixer with a dough hook attachment, add the dough and mix at medium speed for 5 to 7 minutes. (If the dough doesn't come together into a loose ball, add more water 1 tablespoon at a time.) Alternatively, knead by hand on a floured countertop. The dough should be just a bit tacky: not too dry, not too sticky to work with. If you need to add a bit more water (or flour) to achieve this, do so.

Shape the dough into a large ball and divide into 6 equal portions. Gently rub each piece with a bit of olive oil, shape into a small ball, and place on a plate. Cover with a clean dishtowel or plastic wrap and let rest at room temperature for 30 minutes to 1 hour. While the dough is resting, preheat the oven to 425°F. Place a pizza stone, if you have one, in the oven.

When the dough is ready, flatten the dough balls. Using a rolling pin or a pasta machine, shape them into flat strips. Pull the dough out a bit thinner by hand (the way you might pull pizza dough). You can also leave the cracker dough in long strips or cut it into whatever shape you like at this point.

¾ cup semolina flour

¾ cup all-purpose flour, plus additional for dusting the baking sheet

1 teaspoon salt

1 tablespoon sugar

½ cup warm water

2 tablespoons extra-virgin olive oil, plus additional for brushing crackers

⅓ cup dandelion petals, pansies, or nasturtiums*

Cornmeal, for dusting the baking sheets (optional)

Coarse sea salt, for sprinkling the crackers

Set the crackers on baking sheets dusted with flour or corn-meal, poking each with the tines of a fork to prevent puffing. Brush them with olive oil, and sprinkle with sea salt. If you are using a pizza stone, transfer the crackers directly onto it and bake in batches. If you don't have a pizza stone, bake the crackers on the baking sheets. Bake until deeply golden, about 10 minutes, and let cool before eating. The crackers will crisp as they cool.

*   Dandelions are easy to find—the trick is making sure they are clean. If you know where to find a lawn full of dandelions, you should determine before picking them whether they have been sprayed with weed killer or other chemicals, or by animals. Pansies and nasturtiums are pretty easy to grow at home, and many large supermarkets are starting to sell little boxes of edible flowers.

– arctic char –

Arctic char is the smart, well-dressed girl in the corner of the room who's quiet and subtle and doesn't hit you over the head with her confidence, yet everyone in the room (especially her) knows she's got it all going on. Sure, the sexy salmon gets all the attention with her flashy red dress, but that's so very (*yawn*) predictable. When I was first introduced to arctic char, I was drawn in by her gorgeous pink and white dots—her playful summer skirt like a party dress from the '50s.

Arctic char is a chameleon, both a freshwater fish and a saltwater fish. She keeps you guessing. She's tough and can survive in deep, frigid lakes. She can sometimes leave you cold but never bored. Arctic char used to be elusive—a rare fish in the wild—but she's increasingly available down home and local on the farm. Salmon may be sexy, but that char, she's coy and special and dependable: she's the marrying kind.

char with grilled romaine, grapes, and balsamic vinegar

I remember the first time someone told me about a grilled romaine salad. I believe I turned my nose up at the thought. I couldn't get past the idea of cooked warm lettuce. Blech. Luckily, I will try anything once, and I'm so glad I did. Now a whole world has opened up, and that world includes smoking greens like escarole and frisée (see Smoked Sardines with Piquillo Pepper Sauce on page 203). This is a very simple recipe for a late-summer or early-fall evening.

SERVES 4

High-heat vegetable oil, for oiling the grill

3 tablespoons extra-virgin olive oil

1 bunch romaine lettuce, cut through the core into 4 equal portions

1 pound arctic char fillet, cut into 4 equal portions

Salt and freshly ground pepper

4 slices good crusty bread

½ small red onion, sliced into paper-thin half moons (about ½ cup)

½ cup halved and seeded wine or tart table grapes

¼ cup balsamic vinegar

Oil the rack of a grill with vegetable oil and heat it until it is very hot.

With your hands, rub 1 tablespoon of the olive oil all over the romaine sections and the char. Season with salt and pepper. Grill the romaine until it is wilted and slightly charred, 5 to 7 minutes, turning as needed. Transfer to a plate and set aside. Grill the char fillets starting skin side up, for a total cooking time of 8 to 9 minutes per inch of fish (measured at its thickest point). Transfer to a plate, cover, and set aside. Grill the bread and set aside.

Heat a sauté pan over medium-high heat and add the remaining 2 tablespoons olive oil. Add the red onions and sauté for 5 to 7 minutes, or until the onions are caramelized. Add the grapes and balsamic vinegar, and cook until the vinegar evaporates, 2 to 3 minutes.

Spoon the onion-grape mixture over the grilled fish and romaine, and serve with the grilled bread.

PAIRING: A Soave Classico, such as Inama Vigneti di Foscarino 2008, Veneto, Italy, or a vernaccia.

char with roasted cauliflower and apple-vanilla vinaigrette

One night at a restaurant, I was served a single scallop with a butter sauce made with vanilla bean. I remember staring at the little flecks of vanilla seed and secretly dragging my finger through the sauce, thinking that I would have never thought vanilla would pair so well with seafood. But it really worked. When developing recipes for this book, I found that the sweetness of the vanilla needs to hang on something to keep the dish from becoming cloying—and that is where an earthy hook comes in here with the cauliflower. This dish demands a chilly fall evening when cauliflower is in season and you have a bowl of local apples to pick from.

SERVES 4

To prepare the vegetables, preheat the oven to 400°F.

Line a sheet pan with parchment paper. Cut the head of cauliflower in half. Cut one of the halves into ¼-inch slices (reserving the other half for the purée). Spread the cauliflower slices, apple, and onion on the sheet pan. Drizzle with the olive oil, then sprinkle the salt and pepper over the top. Roast in the oven for 20 minutes, or until the cauliflower browns on one side. Remove from the oven and toss with the parsley. Set aside and keep warm.

To prepare the cauliflower purée, bring a medium pot of water to a boil. Salt the water generously and then cook the reserved cauliflower half until tender, 10 to 15 minutes. Drain the cauliflower, chop it coarsely, and purée it and the milk in a food processor or blender until very smooth. Season the purée to taste with salt and pepper, starting with ¼ teaspoon salt and adding more if necessary. Transfer the purée to a bowl, cover with foil, and keep warm.

To prepare the vinaigrette, add the apple juice, clam juice, vanilla bean and seeds, vermouth, and apple cider vinegar to a small saucepan. Bring to a boil and simmer until the liquid

For the vegetables:

1 head cauliflower, stemmed

1 cup medium-diced apple, peel left on

½ small red onion, cut into half moons (about ½ cup)

1 teaspoon extra-virgin olive oil

¼ teaspoon salt

¼ teaspoon freshly ground pepper

¼ cup chopped fresh Italian parsley

For the cauliflower purée:

Reserved cauliflower half

2 tablespoons milk

Salt and freshly ground pepper

For the apple-vanilla vinaigrette:

¼ cup apple juice

¼ cup clam juice

½ vanilla bean, sliced lengthwise down the middle, seeds scraped

¼ cup dry white vermouth

2 tablespoons apple cider vinegar

3 tablespoons extra-virgin olive oil

For the arctic char:

1 pound arctic char fillet, skin on, cut into 4 equal portions

Salt and freshly ground pepper

1 tablespoon high-heat vegetable oil

— sardines —

When the last large sardine cannery in the United States, Maine's Stinson Seafood, shut its doors in 2010 after 135 years of operation, our country's culinary relationship with the sardine was threatened, but it did not die. In just the last year, there has been a resurgence in the collective attention on the silvery little fish. Lots of the excited talk circles around the healthful qualities of the sardine: it's high in protein, high in omega-3 fatty acids, and extremely low in mercury and other pollutants. That's all good news, but what gets me excited about the humble sardine is its incomparable flavor.

When the rain finally abates in the Pacific Northwest (late spring or early summer), fresh sardines start appearing at one of my favorite fish shops in Seattle, Mutual Fish. I head there with the unbounded glee of a kid in a candy store, but first I call my friends to rally the troops. It's a special, fleeting time of the year: as with many fish, sardines have a short season. The ones we see on the West Coast usually hail from California, and they are fabulous and flashy in their own way, light glinting off their silvery flanks. My friends and I snatch them up and meet up later for dinner; some of the sardines get smoked, some pan-fried, others grilled. It's fresh sardine season in Seattle—the silver eagle has landed.

WHAT MAKES THIS A GOOD CHOICE: Wow, let me count the ways. Sardines are extremely low in mercury and PCBs, high in omega-3 fatty acids, and once again abundant—and through good management should remain so. (Though be aware: Scientists have shown sardines and anchovies experience a natural boom-and-bust cycle every thirty to forty years due to oceanic conditions and water temperature.) The Monterey Bay Aquarium's Seafood Watch places sardines on its "Super Green" list—the Academy Awards of sustainable seafood. To be selected, a fish must already be on the Seafood Watch's "Best Choice" list, have at least 250 milligrams of omega-3s in an 8-ounce serving, and contain low levels of mercury (less than 216 ppb) and PCBs (less than 11 ppb). Congratulations, humble silvery sardine: you got yourself an Oscar.

BY ANY OTHER NAME: Sardine (*Sardinops sagax*) is also called pilchard or *iwashi* (in sushi bars).

SEASON: The season depends on when the various sardine stocks travel up the Pacific Coast, but generally, prime season is January through August (with some fresh sardines still available into October). Of course, canned are available year-round.

BUYING TIPS: Fresh sardines are incredible and knock-your-socks-off delicious, but they are also delicate little flowers and don't have the shelf life of other, sturdier species. You'll want really, really freshly caught sardines: three days out of the water max—maybe four if they were handled very well.

QUESTIONS TO ASK BEFORE YOU PULL OUT YOUR WALLET: Are these Pacific Coast sardines? Again, management around the world is not as strict as U.S. management, so it's better—for many reasons—to buy domestic. Where and when were they caught?

CARING FOR YOUR GOOD FISH: Because fresh sardines are especially perishable, keep them very, very cold and eat them the day you buy them.

HOW THIS TYPE OF SEAFOOD IS RAISED OR HARVESTED: Sardines are generally harvested by purse seining, which carries with it very little risk of bycatch. Gill-netting and midwater trawling are other ways sardines can be caught.

....

SUSTAINABLE SUBSTITUTES: Anchovies are a good stand-in, though keep in mind they are smaller, more intensely flavored, and when canned or tinned, much saltier. Mackerel is another good substitute.

dad's sardines on crackers with caramelized onions

1 (4-ounce) tin sardines, canned in extra-virgin olive oil

1 tablespoon dried currants

1 tablespoon gin

½ cup small-diced red onion

Pinch of salt

1 tablespoon extra-virgin olive oil

Freshly ground pepper

Dijon mustard, for spreading on crackers

2 tablespoons finely chopped fresh Italian parsley

I was raised by a committee of loving folks consisting of the chair (my dad), co-chairs (my grandparents), and board members (my aunt and our "housekeeper" Louise, who did so much more than just keep house). Louise is Jamaican, and friends used to tell me that I had a slight Jamaican accent when I was a kid because she was one of my constant companions. Apparently, as the story goes, Louise misinterpreted a story my dad told her about a trip to England where he was served kippers for breakfast. I think she thought my dad wanted that, and so, occasionally, I'd be woken up by the smell of fish frying in a pan at 6:30 a.m. Sometimes it would be sardines for breakfast. I don't think my dad had the heart to tell her he liked littlefish—but not with his morning coffee. This recipe goes out to Louise with love, wherever she may be (on earth or beyond), and to my dad, who raised me to be a good eater and stuck with me through the picky years.

SERVES 6 TO 8 AS AN APPETIZER

Remove the sardines from the tin, discarding the oil, and place them in a bowl. Get the currants drunk by floating them in the gin.

Caramelize the onions by cooking them, along with the salt, in the olive oil in a small sauté pan over medium-high heat. Keep cooking them until they get very soft and light brown. If they get too dry, add some water to prevent them from burning. It should take 15 to 20 minutes for the onions to get good and sweet.

OK, you're in the home stretch now—just mash up those sardines with a fork, add the drunk currants and the caramelized onions, and season generously with pepper. Eat the sardines on crackers with Dijon mustard and the parsley garnish. If you're really cool, you'll eat them for breakfast, like my dad did.

PAIRING: A vermentino, such as Antinori 2007, Bolgheri, Italy, or a rosé.

white bean and sardine salad with fried eggs

This recipe makes use of humble ingredients that can be picked up, last I checked, at a gas station. There is really nothing gourmet about them—in fact, for not much money, a tin of sardines, a can of beans, an egg, and some bread make for an extremely simple and healthful meal. I have prepared this recipe for sworn "sardine-haters," and well, expect to hate no more.

SERVES 4

2 tablespoons red wine vinegar

¼ small red onion, cored, sliced into paper-thin half moons (about ¼ cup)

1 (4-ounce) tin sardines, canned in extra-virgin olive oil

2 tablespoons sherry vinegar

2 cups bread cubes

3 tablespoons extra-virgin olive oil

Salt and freshly ground pepper

1 cup cooked white beans (canned is OK)

¼ cup chopped fresh Italian parsley

4 eggs

Butter, for frying the eggs

¼ cup Parmigiano-Reggiano curls (made using a vegetable peeler)

Preheat the oven to 400°F.

Pour the red wine vinegar over the onions. Let them pickle at room temperature for at least 30 minutes (1 hour is better), stirring occasionally. When the onions are done, drain them, squeezing out any liquid and reserving it for other uses.

Remove the sardines from the tin, discarding the oil, and place them in a bowl. Pour the sherry vinegar over the sardines and let them hang out for a bit while you make the croutons.

In a large bowl, toss the bread cubes with 2 tablespoons of the olive oil and then season to taste with salt and pepper. Spread the croutons on a baking sheet and bake them in the oven for 10 to 12 minutes, or until they are crisp and lightly browned. Set aside.

Drain the sardines and pour the vinegar into a big bowl with the croutons, beans, and parsley, reserving the sardines. Add the remaining 1 tablespoon olive oil to the bowl. Season to taste with salt and pepper. Place the salad on a platter.

Fry the eggs in a hot skillet with a little bit of butter, but leave the yolks runny. Top the salad with the pickled red onions, reserved sardines, fried eggs, and Parmigiano-Reggiano.

PAIRING: A verdelho, such as Rafael Palacios Louro Do Bolo, 2007, Galicia, Spain, or a vinho verde.

skillet sardines with fennel, currant, and pine nut salad

There is a special place in my heart for this recipe. It started with an idea: could I transport an eater to the Mediterranean with just a bite? One bite. I knew I needed a very fresh fish, a fish not normally cooked here in the United States, an underdog fish that deserved its day in the sun. I took the humble sardine and started with a list of ingredients, crossing them off one by one until, hopefully, I distilled—in one bite—a sidewalk café baked in the sun and a Mediterranean breeze that makes you tuck your hair behind your ear and carries with it the faintest hint of the ocean.

SERVES 4

To prepare the sardines, rinse them under cold running water and, with your fingernail, scrape off any scales. Starting with one sardine, gently bend the head back and remove it. Place the sardine on a cutting board. Use a sharp knife or scissors to cut a slit along the belly line, starting at the top and cutting all the way to the tail (without piercing the back).[‡] Rinse the cavity under running water to remove the innards. Place the sardine back on the board, with the open cavity facing you, and carefully cut into it, splitting it open like a book, being careful not to cut through to the other side. Once you have opened the sardine, carefully—with your fingers—pry the spine and rib bones out, leaving as much flesh on the fish as possible. (Don't worry too much about small bones because the high-heat cooking will make them so tender you won't even notice them.) Cut or pull off the tail, along with any attached bone. With scissors, snip off the dorsal fin on the top of the fish. Repeat with the remaining sardines.

Season the inside of each sardine with salt and pepper and tuck in some mint, squeeze some lemon juice over the fish, fold the sides over, and secure it closed with a toothpick. Set aside.

To prepare the salad, heat a medium sauté pan over medium-high heat. Add the olive oil and, when it is hot, add the shallots

For the sardines:

½ pound whole fresh sardines

Salt and freshly ground pepper

¼ cup fresh mint leaves, cut into ribbons (reserve 1 tablespoon for the salad)

Juice of 1 medium lemon (about 3 tablespoons)

Toothpicks, for securing the sardines

For the fennel, currant, and pine nut salad:

1 tablespoon extra-virgin olive oil, plus additional for drizzling

½ cup thinly sliced shallots

Pinch of salt

2 tablespoons toasted pine nuts

½ fennel bulb, shaved thin, fronds reserved for garnish

1 tablespoon currants

1 teaspoon lemon juice

Freshly ground pepper

1 tablespoon high-heat vegetable oil

Crusty artisan bread, for serving

with the cornmeal. Fry the cauliflower for 2 to 3 minutes, or until the florets are browned and crisp-tender in the middle. Remove with a slotted spoon to a paper-towel-lined plate. Add the capers and fry just until they "bloom" open (you'll see the sides wing out, and the capers will start to brown). Set aside.

To prepare the sauce, add the *piquillo* peppers, sherry vinegar, cayenne, smoked paprika, olive oil, and reserved smoked tomatoes to the bowl of a food processor. Purée until very smooth and season to taste with salt and pepper.

To serve, ladle some *piquillo* pepper sauce on each of 4 plates, lay some smoked escarole over the top, and place a smoked sardine on the escarole. Top with fried cauliflower pieces scattered on and around the fish. Garnish with the fried capers.

* Jarred *piquillo* peppers can be found online, at gourmet markets, or at Spanish markets.

‡ Go to www.goodfishbook.com for a demonstration of how to butterfly and debone a sardine.

PAIRING: A sparkling rosé, such as Lucien Albrecht Cremant d'Alsace Brut NV, Alsace, France, or a sauvignon blanc.

– squid –

Squid is one of those galvanizing types of seafood. It has its share of lovers and haters, and for the most part, the hater camp is stocked with the poor folks who've had to chew through overcooked squid better served as projectile weapons. The lovers—myself included—have tasted the divinity found in a piece of grilled or wok-seared squid that has been removed from the flame with the urgency and focus one would employ if their own hand was on fire. Like many, I stumbled through several years wondering why these rubbery rings were worthy of menu real estate until a trip to Italy where, at the famous restaurant Guido da Costigliole, a Michelin one-star restaurant in Piedmont, I was served a bowl of squid that changed my perspective forever. I can only guess at its preparation, but it seemed to be poached in butter that had been flavored with fresh bay leaves. It was insanely good. The squid was so surprisingly tender. I heard my teeth meet with too much force, so prepared was my mouth to do battle. I went back to the same restaurant the next night. I ordered the exact same dish.

quick squid with red chile sauce and herbs

This is the recipe to make for people who are convinced that healthy food can't be made quickly and inexpensively. In no time, the table will be overflowing with fresh herbs, lettuce, and quickly seared salty-sour squid. You can tell your guests to place all the ingredients in a piece of lettuce before dipping into the sweet chile sauce or, alternatively, make themselves a salad and use the sauce as dressing.

SERVES 4 FOR LUNCH OR AS AN APPETIZER

In a large bowl, combine the squid with the fish sauce, lime juice, green onions, salt, and pepper. Set aside while you heat a wok or large sauté pan over high heat. Decoratively assemble the lettuce, cilantro, Thai basil, carrots, and a bowl of chile sauce on a large platter.

Add the vegetable oil to the wok over high heat and, when it is hot, add the squid. Cook, stirring constantly, for 2 to 3 minutes only, just until the squid ring edges curl up a bit and turn white. Transfer the squid to a bowl, leaving the liquid in the wok. Reduce the liquid down to a thick glaze (making sure to add any juices that accumulate at the bottom of the bowl the squid is resting in), about 5 minutes. Pour the glaze back over the squid and serve it on the platter with the accompaniments.

* Thai sweet chile sauce is easy to find in the Asian foods aisle of any large supermarket.

PAIRING: A riesling, such as Navarro Vineyards 2008, Mendocino, California, or a gewürztraminer.

1 pound cleaned squid, tubes cut into rings and tentacles cut in half lengthwise

1 tablespoon fish sauce

1 tablespoon freshly squeezed lime juice (about ½ lime)

2 green onions, minced

Pinch of salt

Heaping ¼ teaspoon freshly ground pepper

1 head butter lettuce, washed and dried, whole leaves picked off the stem

2 cups fresh cilantro leaves

1 cup fresh Thai or regular basil leaves

1 carrot, grated or cut into fine julienne, or 1 cup bean sprouts

1 cup Thai sweet chile sauce,* such as Mae Ploy brand

1 tablespoon high-heat vegetable oil

squid with chickpeas, potatoes, and piquillo peppers

1 (15-ounce can) chickpeas, drained and rinsed

1½ tablespoons plus ¼ cup extra-virgin olive oil, plus additional for garnish (a really nice, fruity olive oil works well here)

½ teaspoon smoked bitter-sweet or sweet paprika

Heaping ¼ teaspoon freshly ground pepper

Salt

1 small leek

⅓ pound small-diced Yukon Gold potatoes, skin left on

⅛ teaspoon cayenne

⅓ cup *piquillo** or roasted red peppers, sliced into ¼-inch rings

¼ cup manzanilla* or other flavorful, cured olives, pitted and roughly chopped

½ teaspoon minced fresh thyme

1½ tablespoons good-quality sherry vinegar

1 pound cleaned squid, tubes cut into ¼-inch rings and tentacles cut in half lengthwise, or whole squid,‡ cleaned and cut

1 tablespoon roughly chopped fresh Italian parsley, for garnish

Squid and potatoes have a fabulous affinity for one another. When potatoes are browned a bit and cooked together, even briefly, with squid, they act as flavor sponges, soaking up any juices and providing a fluffy contrast to the tender toothsomeness of the perfectly cooked squid. When good extra-virgin olive oil and piquillo *peppers are added, you are transported right to Spain—standing shoulder to shoulder at a tapas bar drinking wine out of little cups, the sun hitting your shoulders and music playing. I haven't yet been to Spain, but didn't that sound awfully convincing?*

SERVES 4 FOR LUNCH OR AS AN APPETIZER

Preheat the oven to 450°F.

On a baking sheet, toss the chickpeas with 1½ tablespoons of the olive oil, smoked paprika, and pepper. Season to taste with salt. Roast for about 10 minutes, or until the chickpeas are browned. Set aside. Leave the oven on.

Prepare the leek by cutting off the dark green tougher part (you can save it to make stock). Cut off the root end. Cut the leek in half lengthwise and wash well. Slice into ½-inch half-moons.

In a medium sauté pan over medium-high heat, add ¼ cup of the olive oil and, when it is hot, add the potatoes, a large pinch of salt, and cayenne. Cook the potatoes until they are crisp on the outside and tender on the inside, 6 to 7 minutes. Add the leeks and sauté for 3 to 4 minutes, or until they are soft. Add the peppers, olives, thyme, and sherry vinegar, and sauté for another few minutes. Pull the pan off the heat and immediately add the squid and chickpeas. Mix well and scoop the mixture into 4 small oven-safe dishes, such as Spanish *cazuelas* or medium ramekins. Place the dishes on a baking sheet and bake for 5 minutes, or until the squid is tender and cooked through.

Remove from the oven and garnish with the parsley and a drizzle of good olive oil, about 1 teaspoon per person. Serve immediately.

*   Jarred *piquillo* peppers and manzanilla olives can be found online, in stores specializing in Mediterranean ingredients, or in Spanish markets.

‡   If using whole squid, go to www.goodfishbook.com for a demonstration of how to clean and cut up a squid.

PAIRING: A vinho verde, such as Casal Garcia Branco White 2009, Portugal, or an albariño.

grilled squid with tamarind and orange

Primum non nocere. *First, do no harm. All medical students are taught this, and I am of the opinion that it should also be taught in culinary schools. In medicine, sometimes the cure can do more damage than the sickness, and similarly, overzealous culinary students and chefs can sometimes do more damage to food than if they had simply let the poor ingredient be. I'm a big fan of sauce, don't get me wrong, but some foods shine the brightest when prepared the most simply. Great ingredients don't require heroic culinary interventions.*

SERVES 4

....

Combine the shallot, ginger, chile, orange zest, 2 tablespoons of the orange juice, tamarind paste, salt, and 1 teaspoon of the olive oil in a small bowl. Pour over the squid and let it marinate for 30 minutes.

Preheat an indoor or outdoor grill to high heat. When the grill is very hot, oil the grates well with the vegetable oil and place the squid tubes and tentacles on the grates (you may need to do this in two batches). Weigh the squid pieces down with a cast-iron skillet (or similar heavy heatproof pan). Grill for 1½ minutes, or until you see grill marks. Flip the squid and weigh it down again with the skillet; grill for another 30 seconds to 1 minute. Transfer the grilled squid to a platter and repeat with the remaining squid pieces.

To serve, lay the grilled squid out on a small platter and drizzle with the remaining 1 tablespoon olive oil and orange juice. Garnish with the mint and some sea salt.

‡   Go to www.goodfishbook.com for a demonstration of how to clean and cut a squid.

PAIRING: An albariño, such as Abacela 2009, Umpqua Valley, Oregon, or a grüner veltliner.

1 teaspoon minced shallot

1 tablespoon grated fresh ginger

1 tablespoon minced serrano chile (seeds left in)

1 small orange, first zested, then juiced (about 1 teaspoon zest and 3 tablespoons juice)

2 teaspoons tamarind paste or lemon juice

½ teaspoon salt

1 teaspoon plus 1 tablespoon extra-virgin olive oil

1 pound whole squid,‡ cleaned, tentacles cut from the tubes

High-heat vegetable oil, for oiling the grill

1 teaspoon minced fresh mint, for garnish

Maldon or gray sea salt, for garnish (optional)

chorizo-and-apple-stuffed squid with sherry pepper sauce

For the chorizo-and-apple-stuffing:

2 tablespoons extra-virgin olive oil

3 ounces Spanish chorizo, cut into small dice

¼ cup small-diced leeks, white and light green parts only

½ cup small-diced Granny Smith or other tart green apple

Pinch of salt

⅛ teaspoon cayenne

1 teaspoon tangerine zest (from 1 large tangerine)

2 tablespoons red wine

For the sherry pepper sauce:

1 tablespoon diced shallot

½ teaspoon fresh thyme leaves

Salt

½ cup *piquillo* peppers*

¼ cup extra-virgin olive oil

¼ teaspoon honey

1 teaspoon sherry vinegar

For the squid:

½ pound cleaned whole squid tubes‡

Toothpicks, for securing squid

2 tablespoons extra-virgin olive oil

For serving:

Crusty bread

Recipes are the currency of chefs. My conviction is that when chefs share recipes and ideas with each other, they spread goodwill and foster creativity and collaboration. Thanks to chef Ashlyn Forshner for this fabulous, original, and unforgettable stuffed squid dish, spicy and savory with Spanish chorizo, sweet with apples and leeks, and tart with a sherry-vinegar-laced pepper sauce.

SERVES 6 AS AN APPETIZER

To prepare the stuffing, heat the olive oil over medium-high heat in a large skillet. Add the chorizo and cook for 5 minutes, or until crispy and brown around the edges. Add the leeks, apples, salt, cayenne, and tangerine zest and sauté for 3 to 4 more minutes, or until the apples soften. Turn the heat up to high and deglaze the pan with the red wine until all the liquid evaporates, about 2 minutes. Let the mixture cool for 5 minutes.

To prepare the sauce, add all of the ingredients to the bowl of a food processor and blend thoroughly, stopping occasionally to scrape down the sides. Check seasoning and set aside.

To prepare the squid, using a small spoon, stuff a squid tube with a portion of chorizo-apple filling, packing it in tightly. Secure the squid closed with a toothpick. Repeat with the remaining squid.

In a large skillet over medium heat, add the olive oil. When the oil is hot, caramelize the stuffed squid, cooking for 1 to 2 minutes, then flipping and cooking for another minute or two on the other side, being careful not to overcook. Set aside.

Serve each guest a small plate with one stuffed squid and a spoonful of pepper sauce on the side. Pass around some good crusty bread to dip in the sauce.

* Jarred *piquillo* peppers can be found online, at gourmet markets, or at Spanish markets.

‡ Go to www.goodfishbook.com for a demonstration of how to clean a squid.

PAIRING: A Vouvray sec, such as La Craie 2008, Loire Valley, France, or an Alsatian pinot gris.

— sustainable caviar —

I can't remember the occasion. The "occasion" seems less important than the way I chose to celebrate it. It was me. A spoon. A glass of champagne. A tiny jar of caviar. But let's get serious—unless you're fabulously wealthy, you and caviar are probably two ships passing in the night. I once had the chance to try Osetra caviar from the Caspian Sea and it was remarkable. (I got a tip from a friend that there was a place you could pay a small fee for samples.) Years later I started learning more and more about seafood sustainability issues, and the thought of eating a generation of wild sturgeon in one bite (and knowing that sturgeon was killed for those eggs) took away my enjoyment.

I missed that little celebratory pop when your tongue presses down on an egg against your teeth. I missed the flavor and the occasion of sharing caviar (or eating it all by yourself). Years later at The Herbfarm, I learned all about sustainably harvested caviar. I tried paddlefish caviar from Montana and farmed white sturgeon caviar from California. On my own, I experimented with *ikura* (chum salmon eggs from Alaska) and trout eggs, and a whole new world of egg popping opened up to me. Connoisseurs argue that the flavor is not the same as the "real" thing (Caspian Sea sturgeon), and that even the word "caviar" is reserved only for the eggs of the sturgeon. I argue that whether you call it caviar or roe or eggs, there is plenty to be excited about flavor-wise with sustainable "caviar" and, as an added bonus, my environmental indigestion is now a thing of the past.

four-star duck eggs

This dish is so close to going whole hog that I might as well wrap it in gold leaf. I think I've used every luxury product there is in this recipe. The most significant aspect to get right is cooking the eggs perfectly, so read these instructions carefully. It's an art, and it may take some discipline and perseverance to undo the way you've probably been making scrambled eggs your whole life. I can't wait for you to experience these soft, tiny, pillowy curds of golden goodness set off—just so—by the microscopic popping action of caviar beads between your teeth.

SERVES 4 AS AN UNFORGETTABLE BRUNCH

....

Heat a large pan (pick one that doesn't have a bad reputation as a "sticker") over medium-high heat. Add the butter. Let it bubble, then turn the heat down to medium low. In a medium bowl, whisk the cream into the eggs, and pour the mixture into the pan. Season with truffle salt and pepper. Grab a wooden spoon and start stirring. You will be tempted to turn the heat up, but don't. If you keep stirring the eggs at a medium-low temperature they will produce the creamiest, most delicious curds you've ever had. It should take about 10 minutes before they start to set into small curds, but they will still have lots of moisture. Look for creamy, barely set eggs. Take the pan off the heat. Spoon the eggs into 4 bowls, dollop each with a bit of caviar, and garnish with the thyme.

*   If you can't find duck eggs, you can approximate their richness by using 6 chicken eggs plus 2 chicken yolks.

**   Truffle salt can be found online or at gourmet markets.

*** Paddlefish caviar, as well as the other types of roe featured in this book, is easily available online, if you do not have access to specialty food shops.

PAIRING: A Chablis, such as Albert Bichot Domaine Long-Depaquit 2007, or a Sancerre from the Loire Valley in France.

1 tablespoon butter

¼ cup cream

6 duck eggs,* beaten

Truffle salt**

Freshly ground pepper

1 ounce paddlefish caviar***

Fresh thyme leaves, for garnish (optional)

In a small bowl, mix the sour cream with the horseradish and set aside.

Top each latke with a small amount of smoked trout, a small dollop of horseradish cream, some caviar, and parsley leaves. Serve immediately.

PAIRING: A champagne, such as NV Charles Heidsieck Brut Réserve, or a muscadet.

caviar on buttered brioche with crème fraîche and chives

½ cup warm water (110°F to 120°F)

1 package active dry yeast

3 tablespoons sugar

6 extra-large eggs, at room temperature

4¼ cups unbleached flour, plus more as needed

2½ teaspoons kosher salt

12 tablespoons (1½ sticks) unsalted butter, at room temperature

1 egg, beaten well with 1 tablespoon milk, for egg wash

½ cup crème fraîche, whisked to thicken

1 ounce paddlefish or white sturgeon caviar

1 tablespoon snipped chives, for garnish

You certainly don't have to make your own brioche for this recipe; you could just purchase some and proceed directly to using it as a caviar-distribution vehicle. But, truly, it's very easy to make and doesn't require any special skill (shhh, don't tell French bakers I just said that). With that much butter and egg, it's a pretty forgiving recipe. If you happen to live near a farmers market or know someone raising chickens, the bright orange of farm-grown eggs makes an especially golden brioche.

SERVES 6 TO 8 AS APPETIZER

Preheat the bowl of a stand mixer by rinsing it with hot water. Combine the warm water, yeast, and sugar in the bowl. Mix with a wooden spoon and let rest for 5 minutes, or until the yeast and sugar dissolve (the yeast should show signs of activity after 5 minutes by bubbling up—if not, start over with fresher yeast). Add the eggs and, using the paddle attachment, beat on medium speed for 1 minute, or until well mixed. With the mixer on low speed, add 2 cups of the flour and the salt and mix for 5 minutes. With the mixer still on low, add 2¼ more cups of flour and mix for 5 more minutes. Scrape the dough into a large buttered bowl and cover with plastic wrap. Refrigerate overnight.

The next day, allow the dough to sit at room temperature for 1 hour. Meanwhile, grease a 9-by-5-inch loaf pan. Place the dough in the bowl of a stand mixer fitted with the dough hook, add the softened butter in chunks, and mix for 2 minutes, adding additional flour as needed to make a ball. Turn the dough out onto a lightly floured cutting board, place it in the buttered loaf pan. Cover with a damp towel and set aside to rise at room temperature until doubled in volume, about 2 hours.

Preheat the oven to 350°F.

When the dough has risen, brush the top with the egg wash and bake for 30 minutes, or until the top springs back and it sounds slightly hollow when tapped. Turn the loaf out onto a wire rack to cool.

When cool, cut 4 thin (¼ inch or less) slices, remove the crusts, spread with butter, and cut each square into quarters. Preheat the broiler.

Place the brioche squares on a sheet pan and, watching carefully, broil on the middle rack until they crisp and brown lightly, 1 to 2 minutes. Remove, cool, and top each brioche square with some crème fraîche and caviar. Garnish with a sprinkle of chives.

PAIRING: A *blanc de blanc* champagne, such as Schramsberg Blanc de Blanc 2006, North Coast, California, or a light sparkling wine.

appendix a:
a note on eating raw seafood

I'd like to clear up a few misconceptions. Some people are scared to eat sushi, or more accurately, raw fish. They are afraid it will make them sick. I can understand—I felt the same way when my oldest brother and sister-in-law first tried to tempt me with ruby-red slabs of tuna and meltingly tender bites of yellowtail. "I don't want to get sick," I protested, and they just shook their heads and said, "More for us!"

I'm not a microbiologist, but I would reckon that a warmish bowl of cooked rice left out for hours is more likely to make you sick than chilled raw fish in the cold case or a scallop crudo. One thing people don't realize is that the majority of fish you are served in the raw (with some exceptions) has been frozen before it gets to your plate. This is a good thing—not a sign of inferior quality. You want your fish to have been frozen if you eat it raw because deep-freezing kills parasites. This is especially important with salmon, which is prone to parasites. Please, for your own health and the health of your family, do not eat raw fresh salmon at home. And before you get the notion that you can just throw your salmon fillet in a home freezer for a few days before you eat it raw (or cure it), know this: a home freezer isn't kept cold enough to kill those parasites. If you are going to cure or prepare salmon sushi, buy high-quality fish that you know has been commercially frozen.

The following is taken directly from the Food and Drug Administration's website: "Freezing and storing at −4°F (−20°C) or below for 7 days (total time), or freezing at −31°F (−35°C) or below until solid and storing at −31°F (−35°C) or below for 15 hours, or freezing at −31°F (−35°C) or below until solid and storing at −4°F (−20°C) or below for 24 hours is sufficient to kill parasites. FDA's Food Code recommends these freezing conditions to retailers who provide fish intended for raw consumption." Another misconception? There is no legal definition of "sushi-grade." It is and always has been a marketing term.

While we are on the topic of misconceptions, "cooking" raw fish in acid, as when you make seviche, does not eliminate parasitic contamination. It alters the protein, firming it up and changing the color of the fish, but it does not make it safe to eat. I use commercially frozen and then thawed fish when I make seviche.

The truth is that cooking food is always the safest way to go. This applies to all foods, not just fish. These days, if you are still buying bagged commercial lettuce, you may want to cook that too. I jest, but not entirely. If you are immune compromised, pregnant, or very young, it's important to reduce your risks. Cooking food is a great way to do that. But for the rest of us, eating your fish raw shouldn't scare you—just take appropriate precautions.

It is actually illegal to serve raw fish in the United States unless it has first been frozen. The only exceptions to this rule are shellfish and tuna (as a deep-sea fish, tuna is exceptionally clean and free of parasites). Sushi bars don't advertise this fact because we Americans are pretty hung up on the idea that fresh fish is always superior. My thought is, unless you want to be sick, you'll reconsider this bias. Once you find out your fish has been in the deep freeze, eat it raw to your heart's content, keeping in mind that you still need to keep it cold and safe from cross-contamination, since you are not cooking it. Deliciousness awaits. Much to my brother's chagrin, he no longer gets the lion's share of the sushi.

appendix b:
fish with the highest levels of mercury and pops

I think it is important to alert you to the types of seafood—wherever they may be caught—that are highest in mercury and persistent organic pollutants (POPs).

First, a brief primer on why mercury and POPs should be avoided.

MERCURY

Mercury can damage developing brains and nervous systems; it is therefore extremely important to monitor the mercury exposure of young children, pregnant women, nursing mothers, and women of child-bearing age. Mercury is stored in our bodies and can cause health problems, so even women who are not thinking of becoming pregnant and men should limit their mercury consumption.

Seafood with the highest mercury levels that should be avoided: shark, swordfish, tilefish (golden bass or golden snapper), king mackerel, grouper, marlin, and orange roughy.

Seafood with high levels of mercury that should be limited: saltwater bass, croaker, halibut, sea trout, bluefish, American/Maine lobster, and all kinds of tuna, but especially the larger tunas, such as bluefin, yellowtail, and older albacore. Albacore does have higher mercury levels than the other types of fish I recommend in this book; however, keep in mind that the younger the fish, the less mercury is stored in their bodies. Pacific Coast albacore are caught young, and their mercury levels are lower than those of older tuna caught in other areas.

POPS

Persistent organic pollutants are so named because, to oversimplify, the damn things just won't go away. One type of POP is PCBs, or polychlorinated biphenyls (another is DDT), which are hormone-disrupting neurotoxins that have been banned in the United States since 1977. PCBs are found in high levels in fish that come from polluted waters; they are especially concentrated in the skin and fat of the fish. State health advisories alert residents to avoid or limit eating certain fish from polluted waters.

Seafood with high levels of POPs that should be avoided: farmed salmon (whose feed may contain species with concentrated amounts of toxins) and species from unregulated countries where environmental laws are much more lax.

sustainable seafood resources

RECOMMENDED WEBSITES

Alaska Department of Fish and Game: www.adfg.state.ak.us

Alaska Seafood Marketing Institute: www.alaskaseafood.org

Chefs Collaborative's Seafood Solutions: http://chefscollaborative.org /programs/chef-the-sea

Environmental Defense Fund's Seafood Selector: www.edf.org/page .cfm?tagID=1521

International Pacific Halibut Commission: www.iphc.washington.edu

Marine Stewardship Council: www.msc.org

Monterey Bay Aquarium's Seafood Watch: www.montereybayaquarium.org /cr/seafoodwatch.aspx

Pacific Fishery Management Council: www.pcouncil.org

Salmon Safe: www.salmonsafe.org

Save Our Wild Salmon (SOS): www.wildsalmon.org

Seafood Choices Alliance: www.seafoodchoices.com

Seasonal Cornucopia: www.seasonalcornucopia.com

Seattle Aquarium: www.seattleaquarium.org

Sustainable Sushi: www.sustainablesushi.net

RECOMMENDED BOOKS

Bottomfeeder: How to Eat Ethically in a World of Vanishing Seafood by Taras Grescoe (Bloomsbury USA, 2008)

Fish Forever: The Definitive Guide to Understanding, Selecting, and Preparing Healthy, Delicious, and Environmentally Sustainable Seafood by Paul Johnson (Wiley, 2007)

Fish Without a Doubt: The Cook's Essential Companion by Rick Moonen and Roy Finamore (Houghton Mifflin Harcourt, 2008)

Four Fish: The Future of the Last Wild Food by Paul Greenberg (Penguin Press, 2010)

Sustainable Sushi: A Guide to Saving the Oceans One Bite at a Time by Casson Trenor (North Atlantic Books, 2009)

RECOMMENDED FILMS

Red Gold (documentary directed by Ben Knight and Travis Rummel, 2008)

End of the Line (documentary directed by Rupert Murray, 2009)

index

about the author

When she's not cavorting around the woods picking wild things or combing the beaches for her next meal, **BECKY SELENGUT** works as a private chef and cooking teacher. Selengut graduated from the Seattle Culinary Academy at the top of her class and then cut her teeth working the line at several Seattle-area restaurants. An alumna of the internationally renowned Herbfarm Restaurant, Selengut set out on her own in 2004 to start Cornucopia, her private chef and cooking instruction company, followed quickly by the founding of the seasonal, local foods database SeasonalCornucopia.com.

Once a year, Selengut teaches at the famous Rancho La Puerta cooking school in Baja, Mexico. She also holds year-round classes in Seattle, both privately and for PCC Natural Markets and Dish It Up! Selengut sits on the advisory committee for the Shorewood High School culinary arts program, is a member of Chefs Collaborative, and donates books, classes, and dinners each year to numerous charitable organizations. In between gigs, Selengut carries on a lively, award-winning presence online as Chef Reinvented (www.chefreinvented.com); she is also a freelance writer for *Edible Seattle* (where she was once asked to go catch crabs and write about it) and *Seattle Homes and Lifestyles* magazines. She is a coauthor of the *Washington Local and Seasonal Cookbook*. Selengut lives in Seattle with her sommelier wife, April Pogue, and their two sweet, senile dogs.